FOR THE LOVE OF HORSES

AN ANIMAL COMMUNICATOR'S GUIDE TO HELPING OUR HORSES AND HEALING OUR LIVES

HEATHER GREEN

CONTENTS

DEDICATION

This book is dedicated to horses. With your immense spirit, unconditional love, and undying devotion you have helped, carried, and served us for thousands of years, often thanklessly. May I speak on behalf of humanity in my honor, respect, and appreciation for you, and may this book be a way to give back to you, for all you have given us.

ACKNOWLEDGMENTS

Writing this book was a labor of love that took two years to complete. After becoming completely self-employed, my schedule finally allowed me to sit down and sift through all the wisdom that the horses have instilled in me since they came into my life almost a decade ago. Expressing my own unique truths based on much of my formal and informal education has been a physically exhausting and an emotionally liberating process, one that has brought up my deepest insecurities, fears, hopes, and dreams. Ultimately, the passion of my mission to spread the horses' messages to horse owners and other animal lovers won out over all of life's distractions and any personal hesitations.

I have many to thank for their steadfast support, love, and encouragement, which helped make this book possible. To my dearest beloved partner, Brian, for always having confidence in me and believing that the book would get published. I thank you for hanging in there with me through the long days—and nights—spent typing away at the computer, and for patiently listening to me rant about the importance of getting this book to the people who need to hear it the most.

Much appreciation to my close friend Nancy, for understanding me like no other, and being there for me during my most challenging times. Thank you for your comfort, warmth, and support since the amping up of my self-employment journey at the end of 2009. You helped me get to where I am today, personally and professionally. Even though you are on the other side of the country, our talks make it feel like you are never that far away.

I will always be grateful for the eternal connection and love of my special cat, Rosie. You came back into my life again, at the perfect time—just as I was preparing for full self-employment and musing on the ideas for this book. Your love has kept me healthy and strong, and continues to help me trust. I am so glad you decided to stick around after that last illness.

And to my parents and brothers, whose permission allowed me to share intimate and important feelings and perceptions from my past, as well as certain life events. Thank you for giving me the opportunity to undergo all that I did growing up, for it has helped me be clear about my soul's purpose—helping others heal and grow. Especially to my mother, Peggy: since I've been working as a healer and writing this book, I appreciate your enthusiasm, your unrelenting belief in me, and the happiness you experience with my success. Your wish for my truest contentment has allowed me to be even more successful.

I am grateful to my editor and friend, Julie Simpson, for all your assistance with this book, both with the left-brained logistics and details, and the right-brained creativity and imagination. I am glad that you have been witness to some of my personal evolution over the last seven years. Because of this, you have been able to comprehend the depth and importance of this book, and encourage me along the way. And for all your guidance and support in the production aspects of this book, including every step I've taken to get it to the publisher—I am eternally thankful. I couldn't have done this without you!

I would like to thank Linda Kohanov for being one of the pioneers in this relatively new healing field. Your books, the Epona workshops, and those workshops taught by many who learned and received guidance at Epona Equestrian Services, have inspired and motivated me to follow my life's passion. The first two

Equine Facilitated Learning workshops I attended launched me into the psychic-healing vocation, which has given me the opportunity to make a difference in the lives of many humans and animals. Since then, some of your ideas have formed the basis of my own methods for awareness, healing, and communication between humans and animals.

My gratitude goes out to all who have reviewed various drafts of this book, coached me, or offered feedback, legal and editorial advice, and guidance: Laurel Phillips, Jean-Noël Bassior, Donna Mudge, Laura Kerley, Linda Kohanov, and Cindy Murphree. I also want to thank M. Laurel Stones for offering your artwork for the book cover, and to Joel Anderson, for the great author photo.

For those who have been mentors to me on my spiritual path, with psychotherapy, energy work, intuitive study, or horse medicine, I thank you. All of your tools have been like pieces of a jigsaw puzzle, which when put together create a whole new entity. This original form is what brings multi-leveled healing and transformation for others and myself. I also want to thank the many humans and horses who were part of the stories I shared under a disguised identity. This book wouldn't be what it is without you. Special thanks to all of my human and animal clients for helping me learn and grow. The many healing sessions I have done with you have provided much information for this book.

And finally, to the horses, for just being you. I am truly blessed to know the power of our infinite love. Thank you for calling me to the next level of my adventurous, never-ending journey to enlightenment, and for accompanying me every step of the way. You have helped me find balance in life's ups and downs, and have taught me how to go with the flow. Words cannot express the depth of my gratitude for your part in my healing process, and for all the humans you've served and healed in all times and existences.

PREFACE

On the transformative journey of writing this book, I was consumed and baffled by the riddle of how to portray the profound awareness, emotional unfolding, and life adventures of those in its pages. I spent many hours agonizing over the details. Much of the communication I have with horses comes naturally to me, including the knowledge of what can help them heal, as well as how they can help humans heal—but the process of explaining it in a book that is meant to reach people of various backgrounds was no easy feat. It's like trying to put into words the meaning of an exquisite work of art, or a breathtaking sunset. Such things are felt and understood only by the human heart.

Much of my work with horses is just that. Our culture still values the mind and logic over feelings and intuition. Many of us try to understand the world mentally, and feel more at ease when things fit into the safe box of rationality. Although I have done my best to write about many of the mystical experiences I have undergone while communicating with horses, healing them, and being healed by them, there are some things that simply cannot be translated into words. Metaphors and analogies open a doorway of comprehension for these life events that your consciousness may not grasp but your spirit can sense.

Many of the humans and animals discussed in this book are an amalgamation of particular animal and human clients, colleagues, healers, teachers, friends, romantic partners, and family members—to protect their privacy. I have also disguised these individuals by changing details such as names, locations, timing and duration of events, types of workshops, and other identifying characteristics. In instances where such characteristics could not be adequately disguised, as is the case with my biological family and some of my personal life events, I attained permission to use the information needed to get the healing message of this book out to all who will benefit from it.

The information in Chapter Eight, "Wild Horse Lessons For Humanity," is based on my observing and providing healing services for some horses recently taken from the wild. Some of the information also came from research, but much of it was channeled from the dream horses (the group of horse spirits who have sent me information about horses since I've begun my soul's purpose work). My intent was to share how the wild horse collective, through their living example, can help expand the consciousness of humanity.

It is also important to mention that the information for this book came to me over the course of six years as I spent much time healing with horses, individually and in workshops, and educating myself by researching and reading about their amazing healing abilities. Many of the aspects of the stories and themes scattered throughout this book were originally published in *The Ojai and Ventura View* when I wrote for the paper from 2010-2011. To the best of my recollection, I have given credit to the many people and sources from whom I have learned much, but at this point in my career most of this information feels like common knowledge to me.

I am not a horse trainer, and this book is not a riding or training manual. Although I enjoy riding, I am not a competitive or seasoned rider. Like all riders, I continue to personally grow and develop, expanding my riding abilities with the help of each individual horse that I ride, and in every riding experience. My overall intention is to connect to the horse while riding out in nature, which is my medicine as well as my recreation.

Much of the information and all of the stories shared in this book are based on the life experiences I've had using my natural psychic-healing gifts, allowing me to better understand, connect with, and heal both horses and humans. The stories I have shared where I am riding or doing ground work with a horse are examples used to describe how humans can improve their relationship with their horse, or enhance their horse's health, behavior, and wellness. They are not horse training methods. If you are seeking riding or training guidance, please consult or hire a professional riding instructor and/or a horse trainer. In addition, please be advised that any communication skills, healing techniques, or health recommendations given in this book are not a substitute for evaluation, diagnosis, and treatment from a licensed medical professional or veterinarian for any physical or mental health issues in animals or humans.

This book is meant to be a journey of understanding horses more deeply and relating to them differently. As you dive in and explore with me, I invite you to open your mind to the best of your ability, and leave behind all preconceived ideas or perceptions about horses and humans. Set aside everything you've ever been taught or told about horses for now, knowing you can take back that information after you finish this book, if it still resonates with you.

My intention is to reach a broad audience with varied interests, values, and spiritual viewpoints. We each have our own individual way of perceiving and learning, and preferences for taking in new data. For this reason, the book covers a wide array of topics delivered as stories, research, metaphysical ideas, and channeled messages. I used this style of writing to help each reader fully receive and understand the information from this book that will assist them. In any case, there is something here for everyone. The specific passages of this book that ring true to you, warm your heart, inspire or motivate you are what you are meant to take from it.

On the contrary, if parts of this book push your buttons or trigger you, it might be a sign to look more closely at your own personal issues, wounds, or dilemmas. The many controversial subjects included in this book are meant to help you open your mind, increase your awareness, form new opinions, and take action, which often creates the changes we wish to see in our world.

If you have explicit conceptions based on your religion or personal beliefs that contrast with some of the metaphysical or spiritual information in this book, I hope you'll still ponder applying these methods in your life. Through my formal education and my communication with the horse and nature spirits, I have learned about universal laws and other spiritual ideas that I share here with you because they have proved helpful and healing in my own life journey and with my human and animal clients. I have been pleased with the consistency and accuracy of the spirit messages over time, and they have always been sincere and optimistic in nature.

When considering unfamiliar metaphysical concepts, it might help to take breaks. Continue reading after you've had time to let these new ideas sink in. Ultimately, you must discern for yourself what is truth. It is not my intent to get you to accept my point of view, but to benefit from it. Take what works for you and leave the rest.

Throughout this book, I reveal numerous communication skills and energy techniques that I've learned and used in my experiences with animals and nature. If you are more comfortable understanding and working with these tools in a simple, step-by-step process, Chapter Twelve will give you that opportunity.

Prepare to embark on this exciting, transformative journey that will take place while you read. Beginning anew with a clean-slate mind, we can now take steps into the great mystery of the infinite vessel of magic that exists between a horse and a human. I hope you will enjoy the wild ride as much as I have!

INTRODUCTION

My calling to work with horses came to me many lifetimes ago. I am blessed to have had the privilege of working with these magnificent beings over such a long period of time. But what is important is not the time I have spent with them, in those lifetimes and this one. It is the bond we share, and the love that flows between us. Because of this, I am committed to helping horse owners understand and connect with their horses, leading to better health and happiness for both species. This is true for all animal lovers with regard to the animals in their lives. A healthy, happy horse or animal can help a human heal in unbelievable ways, leading to the greatest success in all areas of the human's life.

I was in the midst of my journey of self-healing and discovery when it all started. After five years of personal psychotherapy, which included regular healings with a shamanic practitioner, I was working as a marriage and family therapist (MFT) intern. I had also worked as a registered nurse for nine years and wanted to learn about the emotional and mental causes of physical illness, as well as what a person could do to transcend suffering and achieve their dreams.

I had my own reasons. I started on my spiritual path almost a decade earlier, which began with reading spiritual texts and visiting healers. On this path, I had been clearing old patterns, traumas, and emotions that had originated before this incarnation and were recreated throughout this life. I didn't know it at the time, but according to Vedic Astrology, I had already begun an eighteen-year cycle of intense transformation called Rahu—one that could help you heal quickly and immensely, but not without challenges and major life disruptions. I was already weary from all this hard work. Like many who have gone through periods of great upheaval in their life, I found myself struggling in relationships, bored with my job, and in conflicts with those I lived and worked with. I will never forget the year I lost my apartment, and almost lost my job and cat, all in just a couple weeks. At times I felt like giving up, but I knew if I did, things would only get harder. It was my personal goals that kept me going—kept me inspired, motivated, and focused on my path of healing. I wanted a healthy romantic partnership, and a career that kept me interested, learning, and growing.

I had always been drawn to the healing arts. During the course of my shamanic work, I became aware that I was a natural-born healer. This was not entirely surprising, because I had always known that I was an empath. Feeling and sensing the emotions, thoughts, physical sensations, and energy of those around me was a common, everyday experience. I was also a nurturer, easily caring for and assisting others with their needs, wants, and overall well-being. Even as a little girl I was already expressing my healing abilities. Following my tonsillectomy at the age of seven, I would line all of my dolls up in a row, and then heal and comfort them. I would pretend they were sick or hospitalized, so I bathed and medicated them, and quietly tucked them in bed. This early play foreshadowed my later work as a nurse.

The shamanic healings I received over the course of five years helped me open up to and understand my healing abilities on a deeper level. In my own healing process, I was learning energetic techniques for healing others. However, I didn't know it at the time. I had no idea where this path was going to take me. I knew the MFT intern work was the right direction, but I did not think it was the destination. It felt too restricting and unoriginal.

It seemed that once someone was diagnosed, they were automatically placed in a box with a label. Although I respected the research and knowledge developed over centuries in the field of psychology and the intention to provide guidelines for practicing safely, I already had an RN license. I did not want to feel pressured to follow more cookie-cutter rules and regulations for effective healing.

From personal and professional experience, I have found that psychotherapy offers the regularity of safe space and support that is needed to help one build up the inner strength to make changes on their own. But as I studied and practiced psychology, I realized that I lacked confidence in many of the ideas and beliefs of mainstream and alternative-minded MFTs or psychologists, both those I read about and those who were my teachers. I also thought some of the psychological methods for healing were outdated, and no longer relevant or applicable given the speed of transformation that was occurring for many on Earth in current times.

I arrived at two conclusions. The first was that something was missing. Something needed to help others heal was unknown to society, or at least to me. The other conclusion was that it wasn't correct to assume the same "treatment" would work for every person. We each have a unique soul, which always needs to be considered in the healing process. We have strengths and weaknesses that stem from past lifetimes; we each have spiritual gifts and talents that influence how we heal.

After coming to these conclusions, I had an epiphany. I was sitting in my therapist's office, confused about where this path was taking me. My therapist said, "Look inside. Ask to be shown where you are headed." I saw a horse. This surprised me, because I hadn't yet been in personal contact with horses, except for a couple riding lessons as a kid that I could barely remember.

It would have been easy to forget about the unexpected image, but then the dreams came. It was a haunting of horses. Over a three-month period, horse after horse came to me as I slept. Sometimes I heard their hooves thundering around me. Other times the call of their whinnying drew me into their barns and stalls, shaking me to the core. I walked into their spaces in the dreams. I would always end up face to face, staring into their wild, anxious eyes. Tears welled in mine as their cries pierced my heart. I could feel the love from them and the love I had for them at the same time, yet most of the time I stood alone feeling helpless. Many dreams ended with me opening their gates so they could run free, or soothing them with a gentle caress across their face or neck.

I had another dream series that was life altering. In each dream, I would always find myself alone in an unknown house. I'd wake up, get dressed, and comb my hair every morning. While brushing my hair one day, I discovered ivory, tooth-like points coming out of my head. At first I denied it, simply thinking it was an old injury or a cyst. I was also relieved that my hair was long enough to cover them up. But with each successive dream, the points that grew from my skull evolved, turning into horse hooves, and later, horse legs. I could no longer deny what was happening, and no longer hide these horse legs under my hair. Horrified and ashamed, I knew I could not keep this secret to myself any longer. I had to begin to accept the truth and let others see me for who I was, even if I was rejected, ridiculed, or ostracized for it.

After experiencing these recurring dreams for many months, I decided to investigate what my path with horses might be. I obviously had some special link to the mind of horses, and even if my gift was unconventional, or made me appear odd or outlandish, I knew the dreams would not stop until I discovered what my role in their lives was. But it was the love that really got me motivated in this unfolding mystery. It was *for the love of horses*. I was meant to help them, and they in turn would be part of the missing piece I was looking for to help humans. This book tells my story of working with horses, how I became an animal communicator, healer, and caretaker, as well as how they have healed my life.

I also share the many reasons and ways horses heal us through the explicit, real-life stories of the humans and horses I've worked with on my journey as a healer. Best of all, this book is my way of giving the horses a voice—making humans aware of their deepest desires and needs, helping to improve their relationships with humans, bettering their health, and improving their overall well-being. May this book call you to let your own love of horses lead the way to a deeper connection to them and to humans. And may this love also be a dedication to your own personal healing and evolution.

PART ONE

INITIATION

CHAPTER ONE

ALL THE LOVE

They say that horses come into your life for a reason, and I have found that to be true. Whether you are a trail rider, involved in competition, working with kids, or living on a farm, you have probably found that horses lend a magic and wonder to your work or play, and even bring solutions to life's challenges in unexpected ways. I know I was surprised when they crossed my path.

I was working as a counselor and nurse when I started to have recurring dreams and visions about horses. These came to me throughout the day and night. The interactions with the dream horses were emotional and inspiring. Their cries rang with urgency and desperation, and I knew they wanted my help and were trying to tell me something. It felt as though I was given some information on a deep level, as all of my physical senses took it in overwhelmingly, yet my mind could not comprehend what it was. I had no idea what to do about this at first, but I knew I had to do something.

While working at the local hospital, I walked into the nurses' station one day and found an open magazine. After all the dreams, I was not shocked to see it was opened to an article featuring horses. These were not your average horses. The article was about horses who helped people with their emotional issues. The method was called Equine Facilitated Learning, or EFL. As introduced by Linda Kohanov in her book *The Tao of Equus: A Woman's Journey of Healing and Transformation Through the Way of the Horse*, EFL is "defined by the Equine Facilitated Mental Health Association as an approach within the Education classification of Therapeutic Riding that also branches into the Therapy component."[1] I was fascinated by the stories shared in the article about how the horses chosen for this work helped people become aware of suppressed feelings, relational dynamics, and spiritual insights. They also helped people be present and grounded in their bodies, in some cases noticing physical sensations for the first time in areas where they had been numb. The article mentioned upcoming workshops. Already working in the field of psychology and searching for a way to help people even more than traditional psychotherapy could, I knew I was in.

My first horse workshop was scheduled for that summer in New Jersey, in a small rural town. I was eager to attend. Fresh with beginner's mind in this work, I was open and curious to whatever I would discover. I knew something big would be uncovered about my own life. At the time, I was estranged from my biological family due to unresolved issues from the past. I missed my mother terribly. It had been three years since we had seen each other in person, or even spoken. I called her about a month before the trip to see if she would be willing to go to a therapy session with me to help heal our relationship. It was clear that we did not see eye to eye on the past, or remember things the same way. But the time wasn't right for us to work things out, and that opportunity to reconcile was lost.

The issues went back to my early childhood, when I hadn't felt validated for my experiences and perceptions. Growing up, I shut down many of my psychic abilities because I didn't think there was anyone around who would understand. I often felt ashamed of my sensitivities and gifts. I assumed my family members would think I was crazy. Clearly, they didn't see what I could see, or everyone would be talking about the ghost that roamed the upstairs hall at night.

I also shut out my psychic gifts because I didn't want to know the reasons behind many of the arguments and misunderstandings that went on between the adults and authority figures around me. I didn't want to know the skeletons in their closets, hidden desires, or secrets they kept from each other and themselves. It was too much of a burden for me to bear—having direct access to another's inner life. I buried the secret knowledge and the many emotions that went with it deep within myself. The only time they came out was when I could no longer keep them down, in the heat of anger. This pattern went on throughout my childhood, and it was up again now in my adult life.

It was time to heal another trauma as well, the loss of a romantic partner. The quicksand of anger and grief from losing my boyfriend, Ken, solidified with the pain of the ongoing separation from my family. Although both the break-up and the separation with my family took place years ago, I was still as raw as when they occurred. These feelings were stuffed inside of me, not yet having an outlet for expression or release. I hadn't been ready to deal with the feelings or reach out to anyone. The distance from my mother was the hardest, because we had always been the closest. Having isolated myself from family and most of the people in my life, I was alone and scared. I decided this workshop was a perfect opportunity to do something about it all.

I arrived at the location of the workshop and a beautiful energy washed over me as I stepped onto a vast, bountiful land of cherry and dogwood trees and colorful fruit orchards. Immediately, I felt the magic and excitement of what was to come; yet I also felt an inner calm. It was the kind of feeling that let you know you were at the right place at the right time. I wasn't sure if the energy I was feeling was coming from the horses or the land, or if it was from both. Either way, I knew this healing force was already working with me, even though the workshop hadn't started yet.

I went into the barn to greet the horses that night before the workshop. They were already looking at me when I walked in, as if they were expecting me. I was drawn to the lead gelding, the wise elder of the bunch. His name was Buck, and he was a dark bay Quarter Horse who lost an ear in a fight in his younger years. Buck was the granddaddy of the herd. He took a few steps closer to me to get a good look.

Buck peered into me. This seemed to be more than just checking out my vibe; it was as if he was trying to place something, doing a thorough internal inventory of my life and deepest self. I felt vulnerable with this intimacy, and took a few steps back. Conflicted by fear and curiosity, I stood there a little bit longer. I felt at home with Buck, and the safety and comfort from this feeling helped me overcome the anxiety I had about what would happen next.

The next morning all the participants lined up outside the barn to prepare to meet the horses we would be working with throughout the weekend. I sat in nervous anticipation, and it was difficult for me to stay focused. My mind kept reflecting back on the intense dream I had the night before. In it, I looked into a mirror and saw my distressed mother. I wanted to reach out and comfort her, yet I was flooded with the conflicted emotions of anger and grief surrounding the estrangement. Then I seemed to drift off as though being taken away by a current, and my mother disappeared from sight.

As we began meeting the horses one by one outside the barn, I already understood their true purpose in providing the healing in this work. At the time, I was still not fully conscious of my gift in being able to communicate with animals, but was blown away by the dignity, nobility, and self-worth some of these animals radiated. I had not seen emotional mastery like this in most humans! It was obvious in how they carried themselves: heads high, but not in fear, and with a clear purpose behind the determination in their strides. In one of the horses, a spunky chestnut Arabian called Lucy, I sensed a vast inner knowing from the reflection of her soul in her eyes and across her face. Seeing this in a horse's face is like regarding those humans you recognize as old souls. They have a wisdom that permeates expressive facial features, and an expansiveness that is palpable through the depths of the sea in their eyes.

Lucy looked over at me and her energy touched me deeply. Tears came when I felt her immense compassion and unconditional love. It was as if I heard her say, "We are here to serve. How can we help?" I knew that she was certain exactly what her role was, and why we were all there. I had an indescribable sense that she was tuning in to what each of us carried inside, what we needed to work on, and how ready we were for it. I can't explain how I knew this, but my heart felt it to be true. I was awed by the dedication to service and level of consciousness this mare had. Up until this point, I had assumed the horses doing the experiential learning work were mostly acting on their instincts. We had not even begun the real healing of the weekend, and I was figuring it out. These weren't horses who only wanted to be in shows, ride down the trails, or graze in the fields all day. With Lucy on their team, these horses were happy to help us heal. This was their vocation.

Most of the exercises and lectures of the weekend were a blur. There was a lot of information shared about how our lives led us to the workshop, what we intended, and why we wanted to work with horses. The teachers explained that these horses had various backgrounds, including trail riding, hunter-jumper, and ranching. In recent years, in every case, they had begun to be bored with, and even refused to do, their usual everyday routines. Like a nurturing caregiver in a family who naturally grows up to make healing a profession, these horses were born to help humans with healing and awareness.

One of the helpers in the workshop, a neighbor of the lead instructor, and Lucy's owner, Kate, had stumbled across Lucy's ability to change the life of humans when she began struggling with depression and her finances years before. Kate explained that miracles occurred because her schedule opened up significantly after she was homebound due to her illness. Kate had more time to spend with Lucy, and in doing so, her lifestyle completely changed. She was no longer distracted by her external life. She had no choice but to slow down, be in the present moment, and feel what was going on inside of her. As Kate continued to face these deep-seated feelings with each passing day, they began to disappear. Profound guidance and insight followed after her long morning walks or trail rides with Lucy. After several months, Kate was able to begin to rebuild her life financially and emotionally for the better.

When the instructors at the workshop first began to discover what is now called Equine Facilitated Learning (EFL), they didn't know exactly how the horses helped people, other than that they were empathic by nature, and like children, would act out the feelings, physical sensations, or behaviors that adults were not completely conscious of. In this way, being around a horse is a good way to also discover if you tend to repress or suppress disliked parts of your personality.

"The name Equine Facilitated Learning was created by the Equine Facilitated Mental Health Association (EFMHA), a special interest section of the North American Riding for the Handicapped Association (NARHA)," wrote Linda Kohanov in *The Tao of Equus*.[2] These organizations were the founders of the practice of employing horses in various therapeutic settings with humans, where they are involved in activities that include riding and interacting with humans on the ground. They have recently merged to form the Professional Association of Therapeutic Horsemanship International (PATH Intl.). Some examples of therapeutic settings where horses work with humans are: facilities for handicapped riding, otherwise known as hippotherapy; Equine Facilitated Psychotherapy, "which promotes personal exploration of feelings and behaviors, and allows for clinical interpretation of feelings and behaviors"; and EFL, which only "promotes personal exploration of feelings and behaviors."[3]

Practitioners of EFL, and other associations, such as the Equine Assisted Growth and Learning Association (EAGALA), have discovered that horses can help humans re-route neurological pathways in the brain, releasing trauma loops and turning old and unhealthy behavior patterns into healthy ones. As Kohanov described through her work with Dianna Hine, M.A., in *The Tao of Equus,* "The brain develops by creating circuitry patterns in response to experience. Severely abused children, to use the most extreme example, consistently associate the feeling of stress with negative, even life-threatening outcomes." When a human is open and vulnerable in a new encounter with a horse, and comfort, contentment, or connection is experienced instead of the old traumas, a "new circuit is created,"[4] a new pathway formed in the brain. Thus, the person can begin to expect to feel fulfillment or joy as a result of upcoming, uncertain circumstances.

BUCK AND TANNER
Ambassadors of EFL

I received the deepest and most profound healing of the weekend in two round pen experiences. For the purposes of fostering freedom and authenticity, the horse chosen for the activity was loose—or "at liberty," as horse people say—during our time in the round pen together. As the horse was free to move about as he or she pleased, I was instructed to have no particular agenda other than to observe where my personal intentions for coming to the workshop would take me in this experience of simply "being" with the horse.

Most people's intentions involved their own reasons for coming to the workshop—for life guidance, healing, awareness of unhealthy belief systems, behaviors, and relationships and how to change them. But I knew mine were more than curiosity about what the dream horses wanted to reveal to me, or how EFL could help people. I knew my intention, whether I consciously wanted it to be or not, was going to involve working out my feelings related to the estrangement from my family, especially my mother.

I felt a friendly connection to Buck, the wise old gelding I had met the night of my arrival. Since he had already taken stock of what was going on inside me in our first interaction, I chose him. I thought working with him would help the session flow more easily, without the awkwardness of introductions.

As instructed during the workshop, I knew I had to be real about how I felt or Buck would pick up on my feelings and likely act them out. But I did not feel totally comfortable expressing heavy emotions around other humans. Even after five years of psychotherapy, I could not easily do this with a regular therapist. The workshop participants were gathered around the round pen, offering safe space and group support, in keeping with the intention of these healing workshops. To ease my anxiety, I tried to convince myself that they were well out of earshot. Then I took a deep breath, and knowing this was my chance, I harnessed my courage, opened the gate, and went for it.

When I stepped into that round pen my whole world came to a halt. It was just Buck and me, in our own universe. All of my self-consciousness disappeared as I dissolved into tears the moment he came up to me. I felt totally present in my body, feeling every sensation, yet there was an observer inside of me as well. This observer noted the long, deep heaves of sobs as they came, as well as the way Buck circled the round pen and rubbed up against my body in a timely motion, just when the sobs would subside so I could breathe and reach my hand out to groom his body, giving me strength.

I didn't know what I was releasing or how this was happening so easily when I had an audience, but I didn't care. A deep part of me wanted to heal. All I knew was that I felt completely safe and contained with Buck. When he trotted over to me as I walked in, I felt his understanding. He was wearing a fly mask that day, so it wasn't that I looked into his eyes and knew, although that was how it seemed. It was my heart that told me he felt my suffering, and I knew he could be trusted. I didn't sense any judgment or expectation of anything in return from him. As I experienced my emotions, he was simply being present with me.

Moving with me is more like it. I was amazed. I watched him zigzag across the round pen in different directions and paces as I processed the pain, sadness, and frustration of my family situation. With his movements, and his one ear standing straight up like an antenna, he seemed to work the energy that surrounded my body, helping to dislodge and release a heavy, dark cloud. And then, in a heartbeat, it was over. Five minutes total, that was it, and my body and mind felt so much lighter.

Back with the others, I reflected on my experience in the round pen. I checked in on a triangle I had visualized in my heart before going into the pen. Instead of the thick blue energy I had seen before the healing, I now saw a sunny yellow light. Many commented that my energy had shifted into a joyful, positive presence. I was also enjoying the blossoming of my psychic abilities. Being a precognitive dreamer, I had always been able to sense potential future events. But now, as I revisited what I thought I heard Lucy say earlier, what I felt Buck relay to me in his movements, and the triangle visualization, I began to consider the profundity of what I was capable of. It seemed that fully experiencing my emotions could very well lead me to reclaim the psychic gifts I was born with.

The night before the next round pen experience, I dreamed the workshop's black Persheron gelding came and sat next to me while I slept. Being touched by his tenderness in the dream, I chose to work with him the next day. His name was Tanner. This time the nervousness that came with doing something new was not present. I easily grounded myself, directed my focus within, and received my intention before going into the round pen a second time. Since the heavy emotions were gone, I was curious about what I would learn this time. I received a simple, yet unfathomable message. Love.

When I stepped inside the round pen this time, Tanner moved much like Buck had, yet with an intoxicating exuberance. I stood there in silent captivation. After adjusting to the enormous joy quotient, I realized the horse was trying to tell me something. He would keep glancing back at me as if to say, "Follow me." I found myself skipping behind him. I didn't know where he was leading me, but it felt like it was beyond the present time and space. It was like we were here in the physical, yet another part of us was traveling some mystical road, on a journey where I was given all the pieces to the big puzzle of how I was going to help horses.

Finally, I stopped in the center of the round pen. To my surprise, Tanner turned on his heels and headed towards me without a moment's notice. I was shocked by his swift move and shift of focus directly to me, and I felt my heart race with alarm. Unsure of what to do next, I picked up the lunge whip that was placed in the center of the round pen for boundary purposes, and held it across my body as a barrier. I closed my eyes, clinging with hope that the presence of the whip would make it clear that I needed space.

When I dared to open my eyes a few moments later, I saw Tanner standing about a foot in front of me, licking and chewing, and looking at me inquisitively, as if trying to figure out what was going on. I put the whip down in front of me, and it drew a line of distance between us. Making a game of it, Tanner started to bite at it, and kick it with his front hooves. In between kicks, he'd look up at me like he had when he was leading me in the beginning, this time saying, "What's this for? Why are you keeping this between us?"

I immediately thought of my relationships with men. I tended to attract men who were emotionally abusive or distant, or who would eventually abandon me. The emotional abuse consisted of belittling, controlling, and manipulative behaviors. I didn't have the awareness that they were like this in the beginning of the relationship, and would often find myself longing for love or intimacy that they couldn't provide.

Sometimes I would attract in a man who was emotionally healthy and able to be intimate, but then fear would consume me. I would sabotage these potential relationships due to the lack of the familiar vibe that came with the unhealthy relationships. Even though the unhealthy relationships caused heartache and pain, it was what I had always known. I carried unhealed wounds inside because of it. Like a magnet, these open wounds continued to attract more of the same kind of emotionally distant and abusive men. After years of experiencing hurt and devastation, I got tired of this vicious cycle and gave up on relationships for a while.

I felt the standoff between Tanner and me also represented some kind of block or fear in discovering what my purpose with horses was. This was unknown territory to me, and even though it was an exciting adventure, part of me didn't trust where it would lead. Both of my careers up to this point, in nursing and counseling, had come to a dead end of disillusionment and boredom. I knew I wanted to provide healing services that could help people faster, more easily and gracefully, treating each individual according to the uniqueness of their soul. Because of this, I realized my new vocation would necessitate the full expression of my own creativity, path of service, and style of delivery. To put it simply, I needed to run my own show, but I didn't yet know what it would look like.

We ended the session in this deadlock. I eventually did walk away, and on my way out of the round pen, I asked Tanner for a hug. He easily obliged. From the moment I stepped out, I realized it was essential that I heal these deep wounds with men—the ones who had abandoned and rejected me, leaving me heartbroken—so I could finally attract a kind, compassionate, and affectionate partner into my life. I also wanted to let go of my fear about the direction the horses were taking me with my life's work. I knew there was always a chance I could get hurt or disappointed, in either of these areas. But I also knew that without taking these risks, I wasn't living life to the fullest. I was hiding behind my potential just to feel safe.

The horses at the workshop taught me that life consists of pleasure, pain, joy, and sorrow, all part of what makes our learning and human experience beautiful and whole. When we incarnate, our purpose is to embrace all of our emotions and fully experience our lives. We might not understand the bigger reasons behind the duality of life on Earth while we are in a human body, but we can at least accept that this is how it is.

By the time I left the workshop, it began to sink in that I had a real purpose and gift with horses, and that in both round pen experiences I had been initiated to work with them. This life transition began when I answered Tanner's call to follow him in the round pen. I felt the intensity of being deeply cherished and appreciated in a way I never had known before, and I knew I would continue to receive guidance as well.

Even though I wasn't fully aware of it yet, my psychic "third eye" was opened in such a way that I could energetically read horses, knowing what was in their minds, feeling their emotions and physical sensations, and understanding them like they were my own species. It was as if I had grown up speaking a foreign language and now had discovered my native tongue. The soulful connection and communication with horses was forthright and genuine, which was something I rarely experienced with humans.

It also excited me that our newly formed partnership was mutually desired. From the ecstatic non-verbals Tanner expressed in the session, such as leaping into the air and letting out a heart thumping whinny, he seemed glad that I would be a translator for horses. I was beginning to imagine all the possibilities that this gift could lead to, like horse whispering or training, but for now I was interested in how the horses could help people in the way that I was helped over the weekend. Because the anger and grief from my family situation had lifted for the first time, I was beginning to consider reconciliation.

I also began to desire a romantic relationship again. As I contemplated this, I reflected on my last relationship. Although losing Ken was overwhelming, a part of me was glad it was over. He and I had not connected on a soul level. At the time we met, I had never even thought of the importance of being in a relationship with someone who had similar life goals or a desire for personal growth and development. He had a good job and good looks, was practical and smart, but I never loved him. I always believed that someday I would. But the relationship was stained and soured by arguments and power struggles.

After this went on for years, we both got fed up, severed what connection we had, and went our separate ways. Looking back now, after all I went through with Ken, I wondered why I had stayed with him so long. I guess I believed in trying to stick things out and make them work. I also didn't believe I would be able to attract in anyone better—and I didn't want to be alone.

Contrarily, it was love at first sight when I met the workshop horses. I knew this from deep in my core through the intense emotional contact we made when I arrived. The love was mutual, and they would never betray or abandon me. I also knew that they would stay in contact with me from afar, helping me in my day and night dreams with what was to come, both personally and professionally. Unlike most humans I had known, I easily trusted what my intuition revealed about the horses. Because of this instant trust and familiar connection and ease, I was reminded of my eternal friendship with horses, the depth of love that had existed many times before my current lifetime. It was a bittersweet memory, one mixed with sadness due to our separation until now, and happiness for our reunion.

IMMERSED IN THE HORSE WORLD
Disillusioned and Disheartened

For months after the workshop, wanting to learn everything I could about horses, I volunteered at a local woman's farm, animal rescues, and a few different therapeutic riding academies in northern and southern California. I had no horsemanship experience at this point. You could say I got thrown into it blindly. At many of these locations, another volunteer would often quickly and haphazardly train me on basic horse care. This was often due to time constraints because many of the facilities were short-handed. On top of that, some of the other volunteers were also fairly inexperienced themselves.

Once I got over the initial overwhelm that comes with learning new skills in a fast-paced environment, I observed the other volunteers and workers at these facilities and the farm. From watching them, I was able to master grooming, bathing, putting on halters and saddles, picking hooves, and leading horses out of their stalls and to the arenas or trails where they would be ridden.

After months of practice, and finally feeling comfortable with basic horse care, I really began to notice what was happening around me. Some of the horses did not look happy. It was disturbing to see the way they lived. Many were housed in what seemed like tiny stalls or paddocks without much room to move around. Some were only turned out to pasture once a week. Otherwise, most were only taken out of their stalls when they gave students or visitors rides. For some, this was infrequent, while I was glad to see that others were ridden almost every day. In the California winter, with its consecutive days of heavy rain, I would find some horses temporarily knee deep in water. If there were other stalls available, the staff and volunteers at the facilities would always move the horses somewhere dry. Unfortunately, there wasn't always extra space because additional stalls needed repair, or they were filled up with horses and/or equipment.

I witnessed moments when staff, volunteers, owners, and trainers at these places would strike a horse when they were not obeyed, often out of frustration or fear in unsafe situations. Lack of time, patience, and confidence were all reasons behind these actions, and reasons horses are still mistreated by even the most experienced horse people. There were times I wanted to report it, but I knew that hitting, especially with hands and not an object, is not easily called abuse by animal welfare groups, and that they'd need to consider the specific circumstances in each case.

I also knew that my perspective of the situation was subjective, and wouldn't be viewed the same way by everyone. These horses were definitely not neglected; they had enough food, water, and basic sanitary conditions. Many were also involved in programs where they were either ridden at least a few times a week or could be adopted out. The owners of these facilities and the farm were often doing everything they could with the resources, time, and staff they had. But it still hurt to know that the horses had to suffer or sacrifice themselves under these conditions, simply because, in many cases, they no longer belonged to a specific human. Even if the old or weak would not make it in the wild, I was beginning to think the young and healthy were better off free. Who were we anyway, to think we could just have horses for our own pleasure or desire, at the expense of their ultimate well-being?

The hitting never felt right to me. It was a rude awakening, what I was observing as I delved into the new world of horse culture. I didn't like it or agree with it, but I didn't yet have the skills to show people another way. Even though I knew I had a strong bond and a special gift with horses, I didn't know if it would be enough to go up against these old, outdated patterns of relating to and caring for horses. I was beginning to wonder what the lives of the rest of the horses in my area were like. More and more it seemed as if the workshop horses were a dream or fantasy, not a real herd of horses that were healthy and happy.

Despite these hardships, I still loved and looked forward to every moment I spent with horses. Because they are such big animals, they helped me feel grounded and focused, fully present with myself in every exchange and interaction. They brought a joy to my life in even the simplest activities, like walking or grooming. I felt like I was one of them. Carolyn Resnick's book *Naked Liberty* contains numerous stories that exemplify how wild horses, being true to their core, will only respond to you from a most authentic place. I know this authenticity is related to the depth of their intuitive and emotional natures. I can relate to this, as I have never been able to be phony. When you get to know me, you get the real deal, and nothing less. I'm not afraid to tell you the raw, at times unpleasant, truth. But I don't hold back on the good stuff either—the kindness and loving.

With the undesirable conditions, the physical and verbal attacks, I could tell many of these horses were not able to be authentic. Many of them were not present in their bodies anymore. This is a psychological phenomenon known as dissociation, when the mind distances itself from physical experiences that are too overwhelming to process. These horses left their bodies due to unsafe conditions, trauma, or boredom. It was like the lights were on but nobody was home, which saddened me. And some of these horses didn't even have lights on. Their eyes reflected only a blank stare, and they walked on without pride, dignity, or a choice.

I knew I had my work cut out for me, but I was still dedicated and enthusiastic about following my calling to work with horses. Because of the profound experience I had at the workshop, I no longer felt drawn to psychotherapy. I even quit my counseling job, because the work with the horses seemed to offer healing at a faster rate and on a deeper level, and I needed more time to learn about it.

The one thing that worried me was that many of the horses I was working with were not as conscious as the workshop horses. I wondered if they would even recognize they were helping humans or if they could do the same quality of healing work. They didn't seem to have the same amount of stamina, drive, and willingness—not to mention self-worth—to perform at the level the workshop horses did.

I also thought that it might be a hefty burden for many horses to take on the role of facilitating this emotional and relational work with humans, especially those who suffered from unfortunate living conditions, emotional neglect, or physical abuse. Before I came to any definite conclusions, I wanted to observe the health of other horses, those that weren't rescued or given away because of abuse, neglect, injuries, or old age. I needed to visit horses at private ranches and boarding facilities, and those horses who lived in my neighborhood's backyards to find out if they'd be appropriate for EFL work.

PERCY
The Dance of Intimacy

I was acquainted with someone who had two horses on a couple acres of private property. After talking over tea one day, Sue invited me up to play with her horse, Percy. He was a beautiful golden Palomino, muscular and trim, with finely chiseled facial features, a flowing, feathered mane, and a tail that reached the ground. I told Sue what I was exploring with the horses, and she encouraged me to find out what Percy would be like at this work. He was mostly retired. She bought him a few years before from a rancher and took him on the trails occasionally. He carried a healthy weight and had clean living conditions, as well as a large pasture area where he spent most of the day. From a distance, he seemed more alive than the horses I had met so far.

When I went into Sue's arena with Percy I got more than I bargained for. The moment I walked in, he came right up to me and looked into my eyes. Unlike the last experiential activity I was involved in with Tanner, where I felt fear with the intimacy, I felt something completely different with Percy. It was a combination of attraction and curiosity. We started some sort of dance. Percy would move one way, and I would feel inclined to move over in that direction. Then we would pause for a moment, reflect, and I would have a sense that he was waiting for me to make a move. So I would move in a different direction. He would follow me. And it repeated again. All of this happened with both of our faces and feet less than a foot away from each other. When I tuned in to my body, I felt a glowing, green diamond radiate from my heart, with feelings of warmth, tenderness, and joy. This was the way love was meant to be expressed!

Then we started touching each other. He would nuzzle my neck and brush his face against mine. I would reach up and caress his mane, face, and neck. We repeated these gestures over and over again, and eventually moved together as one. It was beautiful and exciting, and I could not help but wonder what was coming next. Percy had a plan with all of this. He certainly seemed to be leading me in this active expression, because I would hear his directions in my head.

It mostly went something like, "Yes, now it's your turn. Rub my ears and back. This feels great," which would usually lead to a timeless, deep gaze into my eyes. It was sensual and safe, unlike many of the romantic encounters I had with human men. I felt passion and connection burning between us, as the world around us fell away. We ended the session with a hug. He put his head on my shoulder, and I put my arms around his neck. Then he licked my face. We could not end our date without a kiss!

After exiting the arena, I looked at the time and realized almost an hour had gone by when it felt like minutes. Sue moved Percy back into his stall, and I watched as he ate his dinner, back to being a normal horse. I was pleased to know there were more horses who were happy and healthy. From talking to Sue, it seemed that Percy was in good hands—treated well and cared for. From my interaction with Percy, I was glad to find that, like the workshop horses, there were definitely other horses who were willing and able to facilitate this life-changing work.

But I also intuitively sensed that each horse has his own individual preferences and life history, which should be considered before asking him to do this kind of work. Even though the workshop horses wanted to let go of their old jobs and routines to be teachers in EFL, not every horse would feel the same way. It is up to us to determine how much they'd want to assist in our healing process, if at all. Forcing a horse to take on this role can cause emotional harm; he would likely experience powerlessness due to his lack of control, which creates mistrust of humans.

I began to reflect on what I experienced with Percy. I asked myself, what just happened here? Was this real? I was still in blissful shock from having this romantic experience with, of all beings, a horse! But deep inside I knew every ounce of it was ever so true. I was being prepared for my next romantic partner. As many of my old patterns with men had led to rejection and abandonment, I had avoided future intimacy, due to fear of getting hurt. But because this safe and enjoyable experience was a stimulus for re-routing new neurological pathways in the brain, I could now begin to expect to be accepted and loved while being emotionally or physically intimate with a man. I was grateful for this amazing gift.

As I drove away that day, I observed a luminous, magenta-colored sunset on the horizon. It made me ponder love—what kind of man I wanted, what loving would be like, and if it could really happen. Or did I deserve it? I remembered the shaman I worked with in the past, and that he had told me I had a heart of gold. Back then, I thought I had a load of baggage that obscured this treasure and prevented its radiance.

That evening in the car, I decided I did deserve it, could have it, and intensely desired it. Why else would I have experienced what I did with Percy? I needed to continue to heal myself so I would be ready for the real thing. This meant having the courage, strength, and vulnerability to allow myself to be openhearted. I was beginning to understand that being ready for love means you are empowered enough to handle the risk of getting hurt or disappointed. At any rate, I was getting closer to being ready.

After a period of transformation and growth, it is normal to experience a sense of loss, as the old falls out of one's life to make room for the new. Within a few weeks of this experience with Percy, I was shocked by a turn of events in my life.

Things had not been going well with my chiropractor, Frank, who had been treating me for about a year. In the beginning, in addition to helping with my back, he gave me personal advice that I easily accepted. But over the last few months, I had begun to feel that something needed changing in the treatments, something no longer felt right. I was frequently leaving appointments feeling frustrated, irritable, and confused about what was going on. I became aware of a need to set a personal boundary, because I no longer wanted to hear the advice he was offering me. I had recurring dreams where I brought Frank a plant and was showing him the new, long, healthy stems and leaves. Well, I finally figured out the dream's message. It was time for me to move on to a different form of healing. I had outgrown the treatment, and needing someone else's advice. That's why I was feeling so restless and agitated!

When I told Frank how I felt, he surprised me by not seeing things the way I did. Like the conversation I had with my mother before the horse workshop, I felt the familiar surge of the pain that accompanies disappointment and hurt. It seemed that he thought I needed more time to sort through my conflicted feelings about his practice style, and that I wasn't ready to move on yet. Frank also said that I was resistant to healing, and needed to change this if I was going to get anywhere in life. I felt betrayed by his harsh words, and for a moment I questioned whether they were true.

But then I felt my gut drop to the floor. This was my body's way of telling me something was very wrong, and that I needed to act immediately. After excusing myself from the office without a moment's notice, I went out to the car, cried, and tried to breathe. I was grieving the loss of Frank because I knew I could never go back. He would not understand that I wanted to continue healing, just in a new way. Because of the support and bond we built up, it was hard to let go. But I knew my sanity depended on it, as growth often precedes change.

For weeks following that falling-out, I spent my time journaling, being in nature, and processing the emotions in dreamtime. Unfortunately, it was challenging, as Frank had been one of the few people I'd talk to about a situation like this. I had spent the last few years living like a hermit in the healing process, and I did not have many close friends I could confide in, or, I felt, who would understand.

Because of the speed of transformation I was experiencing at the time, I was going through friends like a bag of potato chips—quick, easy, often without awareness, and with great regrets at the end. It was good that some of the friends left my life, but others I tossed away for any little thing that went wrong. At one point, like with my romantic relationships, I got so tired of repeating this pattern I decided to let go of friendships for a while. And so, because I was also estranged from my family, my hospital co-workers and chiropractor were the only personal connections I had for almost a year.

One day while I was at a local bookstore, a book fell off the shelf. It was titled *I Remember Union,* and is the story of Mary Magdalene and her soulmate partnership with Jesus. In it, the author, Flo Aeveia Magdalena, channeled the spirit of Mary Magdalene. She shared that part of the reason Mary incarnated was to help Jesus in his soul's purpose as the Christ figure. It was a beautiful love story that showed how their union helped both of them grow spiritually as well as fulfill their earthly mission to heal, teach, and lay the foundation for the expanded consciousness of humanity that we are part of at this time in history.

I was moved and inspired by this book, and knew that the different form of healing I needed at this point in my life was the healing from the horses. This healing would allow me to move forward on my path of spiritual growth, attracting a romantic partner with whom I could co-create my life's work. Actively participating in this type of healing process would finally enable me to help people in the ways I had been unable to in counseling and nursing.

CHAPTER TWO

FORESIGHT AND HEALING

My connection to the workshop horses called me back to them. It was time. I had dreamed of them throughout the nine months I spent volunteering and exploring the world of EFL. My dreams would often begin with a knock on the door. I would run to open it and find Tanner or Buck standing there, expectantly. Then they would usually rear up, jump, and kick out with delight, turning back to see if I was following them. In most dreams, I would feel frozen, unable to move, and would stare off at them as they ran away. In the last recurring dream, I was finally able to walk out the door after them. When I caught up to them they told me they were glad I answered, that most humans didn't even hear the knock.

After arriving for the second time in New Jersey, I met up with Kate and her horse, Lucy. We walked over to the property of the workshop's lead instructor, Sally, where the rest of the workshop horses lived. We briefly discussed my intentions for coming, that I was opening up to a new, healthy romantic partnership, a career that involved horses, and the healing and transformation necessary to get there. Kate explained that the horses would be facilitating the session today, and that she would be there to guide me if I had any questions or needed help processing. It was a cold, snowy March day, and Kate grumbled about missing sunny, warm California. She had spent almost her whole life out there and only recently moved to New Jersey. Kate warned me that the horses were agitated and restless from being cooped up inside the barn for most of the past two days because of the weather. When we finally reached the barn, I felt the excitement of anticipation bubble up warmly in my chest. I wondered where this fun adventure was going to take me.

My first assignment was to hang out with the herd in the barn. It was going to be a process of automatic writing and mind-to-mind transmission. Kate instructed me to open my mind by connecting to the horses, and to be receptive to whatever came through—whether it be random thoughts, ideas, intellectual facts or research, or feelings. Then I was to write everything down as quickly and easily as my memory would allow. The horses were all in their own stalls within the barn, and Kate left so I would have the psychic space needed for the activity. I felt like a kid alone in a candy store. All these horses to myself—how much we would discover together! And so we began.

I connected with them intuitively through my intent, and noticed their heads popping out of their stalls. I took that as a validation that they were ready. I pulled out my notebook and started to write. Kate had instructed me not to filter anything, to write down everything that I received no matter how outlandish. The point was to leave the critical judge at the wayside and make room for solutions and insights, even miracles, to reveal themselves.

I started talking to the horses through my mind. This mostly consisted of using my imagination. Up until this point, I was used to only receiving messages from them. I wanted to reciprocate. At first it felt like I was making all of this up. How could I be sure they could understand my human language? But I reminded myself this was all an experiment anyway, so away I went. I told them about my three main intentions, and where I sensed my life was heading. Instead of saying it out loud, I relayed these thoughts to them from my mind.

The answers I received came in like a flood. All three of my intentions—for a healthy love life, a new career with horses, and spiritual growth—were entwined. I knew this meant more than that they were related. There would be some opportunity where I could experience and move forward in all three, and as I progressed in one area, so I would in the others. The horses told me the next stage in my journey involved traveling to England. "England, *England*," they said impatiently. They heavily emphasized the second England as if I hadn't heard them. There I would find job opportunities working with horses in a healing manner, possibly even with children. They also mentioned that a potential mate was there.

In a blur of information-sharing and frantic scribbling, the horses disclosed more details to me. This mate would be someone I would meet spontaneously; I would not have to go out looking for him. He would be involved somehow in nature or with animals, and he would be my best friend. They shared that I could have my own land too, but I would have to take steps to set things in motion. "Just do it," they said. "Just do it."

But what exactly, was I to do? Where in England was I to go? As soon as I thought this, I got a response. "Stay close to the crystals, stay close to water." As for the doing, they said I was to begin bringing humans and horses together for healing.

Specifically, I would be able to help children—gifted children. I didn't have to plan what I would do with them. It was all inside of me, ready to emerge. I could use my creativity as a catalyst for the children and horses, sparking the alchemical process between them.

Interestingly, I did not need any training in this line of work, according to the horses. I felt an initial resistance to this. After experiencing what I did in the round pen during the workshop, I knew how much awareness and emotion could arise in a human during this type of work. Many would need assistance with the ability to ground in the midst of powerful thoughts, as well as help with containing unbridled emotions. There would also be the potential for follow-up appointments, to help people process whatever information or insights about their lives had been revealed or would be revealed in the days after the work with horses. I already had a master's degree in counseling psychology, which gave me an advantage in this area. But I needed to learn more about horses, and how horses responded to or were affected by this work. As sensitive as they were, I knew it was possible that horses could be overwhelmed by too much emotion as well, whether suppressed or expressed by humans.

In addition, I wanted to learn how to secure the safety of a horse in a human's presence and vice versa. Many horsemanship training programs offered standard procedures to ensure the safety of humans and horses working together—ways of approaching a horse, behaviors to avoid in the presence of a horse, certain body areas to avoid standing next to, and the ability to notice and respond appropriately to the body language of horses. Although I didn't want to be forced to operate within a box of rules and regulations like I was required to do in the nursing and counseling worlds, my common sense told me that new guidelines and certifications being created at the time by associations such as Equine Facilitated Mental Health (EFMHA) and Equine Assisted Guidance And Learning (EAGALA) were a good place for me to start to build a foundation of knowledge in this field.

Having confidence and faith in my natural abilities, the horses expressed that I had the talent and passion to get things going, which was all I really needed. And the time was now! The kids needed me. But I would have to be prepared.

The horses told me there were parents out there who would be threatened by this work. It made sense to me. Through the healing power of horses, which involves and accentuates their authenticity and the ability to bring that out in humans, complemented by a child's open and pure perspective, much could be expressed. From my own experience, I knew that kids might harbor anger, fear, or sadness, dislike or rejection of what is happening at home or school, or even an awareness of the secret thoughts, desires, and behaviors of those closest to them. Even the most innocent parent or authority figure is often uncomfortable with anyone, much less their own children, knowing the inner workings of their mind, hidden desires, or private life occurrences.

According to Lee Carroll and Jan Tober in their book *The Indigo Children: The New Kids Have Arrived,* many of the souls being born today and over the last ten to fifteen years are wise, gifted, and highly evolved, beyond those in the generations before them. In Doreen Virtue's books, *The Care and Feeding of Indigo Children* and *The Crystal Children,* these old souls are described as indigo, crystal, and rainbow children, depending on the colors of their auras, their temperaments, and their collective purpose.

As Carroll, Tober, and Virtue emphasized, because of their unique soul attributes, these kids need to be understood, respected, and raised differently than their parents. Virtue explained that some of them need to follow special diets, exercise programs, and be involved in non-structured activities due to their sensitivities and spiritual mastery, which I know can lead to boredom and frustration with current society's laws, rules, and methods of regulation. As well as being extremely sensitive, indigo, crystal, and rainbow children generally have a tenacious will, an unfathomable sense of knowing who they are from birth, and intolerance for injustice or corruption, in any life area.

In one way or another, whether it is through their mighty determination or mysterious spiritual gifts, these kids will bring out the truth of a situation. As Virtue alluded to in her books, the indigos are the fearless leaders, demanding change where law and government are no longer functioning in a way that supports all of society's highest good. The crystal children are the ones modeling peace and harmony, helping to bring together every kind of human and species on the planet, leading to a greater connection and equality between all of us.

The horses told me the majority of those I would be working with would be these special children. And this type of work would be serious business. There would need to be a call-out on abuse. This includes all forms of physical, sexual, and mental/emotional abuse. The horses would draw out from the children all harmful situations—from emotionally toxic living situations, to unhealthy boundaries or sexual behavior, to extreme pressure or expectations in achieving particular educational or athletic goals. Even the potential for abuse would be exposed. The horses wanted me to put my foot down, explaining to the parents how these situations could derail a child's health, well-being, intellectual development, and relationships. In their words, I would need to be "tough as nails," but they had every ounce of faith that I could do it.

Wow. I came up for air. I was surprised by most of the information I was receiving, but it still had not yet fully sunk in. My mind churned with more questions. I wondered about the abuse issues. I had certainly not expected to be addressing these awful life hardships that many children had to go through. How would I even go about it?

But I was also not surprised. Throughout my life, I had experienced emotional pain and violence, which led to feelings of low self-worth, learning challenges, identity confusion, shutting down my spiritual gifts, and difficulty with trust and intimacy in relationships. I had spent many years in the healing process, reclaiming my psychic and healing abilities. I would certainly want these children to be able to retain and amplify their gifts, so they could be living their greatest potential by the time they reached adulthood.

I agreed to think this all over and discuss it with the horses again in the future. I knew that I could continue to communicate with them at any time or place. It was as easy as using my intent and imagination. As I said my thanks and we exchanged vibrations of love, Kate arrived. She asked me if I wanted to share the information I received. I gave her a succinct summary. I told Kate that I wanted time to participate in more EFL workshops for healing and learning. I explained to her that I eventually wanted to get trained in this line of work, but to be competent as a facilitator I knew I would need years of experience first. I still wasn't sure what the horses meant by staying close to the crystals and water. I had a hunch it had to do with maintaining my residence on the west coast and working with the crystal children, but only time would tell.

FORGIVENESS

Although I was thrilled about these upcoming opportunities, I knew there was still an important healing that needed to happen that day. It seemed as though the career doors to working with horses had opened, but the door to the romantic department still needed to be unlocked. I knew I needed something more to help propel me over that threshold.

Standing before the herd in the barn, I felt Tanner's masculine support behind me. Lucy seemed to be pulling, pushing, and maneuvering something invisible in her stall. All of the horses were doing circles in their stalls, moving and pacing in a way that felt similar to what I experienced in the workshop. Because of the uplifting emotional support and the active, catalytic intent behind their actions, I knew they were helping me release energy. I tuned in more deeply to Lucy, sensing that she was doing something else and wanting to find out what it was. As I checked in with my body, I discovered that she appeared to be yanking on a cord from my second chakra or lower belly.

By now Kate was standing by my side, and I turned to her to describe what I was experiencing. In many unresolved romantic relationships, a cord or tie remains, continuing to keep the two people connected on an energetic level. This can continue even if the relationship has been over for some time and both people have not had any contact. For the first time I began to consider why I was seldom attracting men who were open and available for anything more than friendship. Now it made all the sense in the world. There was no room for any other men since Ken because of the lingering attachment, the cord that kept us bound. For a moment I was shocked and disappointed by the thought that I had not dated for years and had been sending out an energetic message to the world that I was still involved with someone.

But I felt empowered and relieved standing there in front of Lucy, watching her indomitably unraveling this old thread from its point of origin. I was more than willing to let her help me break this chain that tied me to the past. As I relaxed into a receptive stance, I watched as Lucy gave one last tug and bit the air in the place where I felt the energetic attachment. In one instant, the cord was cut. I felt excitement dance through my heart as a heaviness left my womb. To think that this had been keeping me from having a love life! Lucy sent me a spiral of unconditional love that wrapped around me like a warm embrace. Like a plug, it filled up where the detached cord left a gaping hole.

Lucy stamped her foot on the ground and left me with an important message. "It is time to claim what is rightly yours. It is time to live your divine blueprint in love." I had missed out up until this time. I could blame it on what had happened between Ken and me, but I knew better. On some level I chose to keep this energetic cord. The relationship hadn't been over for me, because I was still in pain.

Pangs of regret and sorrow brought back old memories. I did not date much in high school, and I always sensed I was not really living life back then. I went out with a few men casually in college, but the relationships never went anywhere. There was usually something missing—the spark, the connection, perhaps the familiar vibe I knew from previous unhealthy relationships.

When I met Ken, just after college, my whole life changed. He was my college roommate's brother. Appropriately sporting the same name as Barbie's sweetheart, he had handsome curly blonde hair and light blue eyes. It was the first relationship I ever took seriously. Even though we lacked the soul connection and common life goals, in the beginning of the relationship he was my closest friend, someone I thought I could share anything with. But as time went on, I began to change. I could not stand up to him or tell him how I felt, which was completely out of character for me. I could not insist that he change his tone with me and treat me as his equal, stop controlling or dominating me.

It was now five years since the break-up, and I still hadn't healed. I was still infuriated and humiliated by the fact that I stayed with him for so many years. How did that happen? As I stood still in front of Lucy's stall, I contemplated and worked through the tumultuous emotions that I still carried from my relationship with Ken—a rich stew that simmered with betrayal, hurt, resentment, and grief. And then I remembered a dream I had just a few days before arriving in New Jersey for this healing.

In the dream, I was reviewing my whole life up until now, in the area of relationships. I was watching it as if it were a slide show. I could see how far back this pattern with men went. The review went in reverse, beginning five years ago where things had left off with Ken, my last real relationship. Then it touched briefly on the shallow, superficial, and transient dating experiences I had earlier in college. Finally, I was able to visualize my lonely high school years.

In remembering this dream, I could viscerally feel the confusion, insecurity, and doubt that permeated my being throughout my younger years. I was terrified of being in a romantic relationship, and assumed it would bring pain or loss. Like in most family, community, and school systems, there weren't many role models for healthy relationships between men and women available to me. Many of the adults I knew were involved in dysfunctional relationships or were divorced. Because of my innate psychic abilities, I knew what was going on in the lives of others. I knew what was happening at home with kids at school, teachers, neighbors, and friends. It all was too overwhelming, and I didn't yet know how to handle my involuntary ability to receive direct access to the suffering of another. Eventually I became hardened and blocked out my sensitivities, including all the psychic abilities that went with them. Deep down, I didn't think anyone would understand my feelings or validate my perceptions, so I never shared what I was going through.

That's when it finally hit me. Standing right there in Lucy's stall—that's when it all made sense. As a child, because of my gifts, I saw and knew things about people that were invisible to others. That's why no one else remembered things the way I did. They didn't know.

Held and protected by Lucy's energy, I realized the key was compassion. I knew I had to release the pain, longstanding resentments, and any needed validation from others if I wanted to move on with my life. As I transmuted these heavy energies and started to feel compassionate, I understood that anyone who causes suffering will have to deal with their own demons at some point, even if it's not during this life. I could relate to another's resistance to heal, because there was a time when I wouldn't have been able to face the fact that I was in a dysfunctional relationship with Ken. Through psychotherapy, shamanic work, and EFL, I discovered that I could not only overcome denial, but also move through and eventually transcend the emotional pain as well, so I knew it was possible for anyone else to do the same.

Shortly after finishing the one-on-one interaction with Lucy, I began experiencing what felt like forgiveness. For me, this was about letting go. Before the horse workshop, I didn't think I could let any of these old experiences and feelings go. But now I knew I could. With this new beginning, I wouldn't need to hold anything from my younger years against my family or Ken.

For the first time in my life, I felt neutral. I could now finally look back on my life *without* feeling the familiar twinges of pain—no more grudges. I knew that finally being at peace would allow me to attract other peaceful and compassionate people into my life, releasing the old patterns and emotions that created the same kind of pain, over and over again. If I was loyal, true, respectful, and honest with myself, I would get more of the same in my life, and this is what I had spent most of my life waiting for.

Before I left New Jersey, Kate and I had a closing discussion. Throughout this day of healing, I was able to get clarity about the bigger picture of my life, and what steps to take next. I had the option to get training in EFL and begin the journey to finding my mate. When I let go of that energetic cord with the help of Lucy, I was letting go of an old attachment that kept me imprisoned. Not only was I finally able to resolve my relationship with Ken, but I was also able to release the painful emotions that kept me separated from my family. Reconciling with them now seemed possible. I felt lighter and free, and I knew I'd be able to move on to the next stage of my life.

CHAPTER THREE

WHAT HORSES WANT

In the weeks following the day with the horses in New Jersey, when I got back to California, I began looking into other workshops and training programs in EFL—programs that focused on working with humans and horses on the ground, not in the saddle. This was a completely new vocation. From talking with Kate and researching this healing field, I knew this type of work wasn't something I could begin facilitating after just one workshop experience, or even after receiving a formal training. After all, I was still new to horses, at least in this life.

I also began to realize the importance of taking some formal riding lessons. I wanted to experience the joy and skill of riding, and to understand more about horses through connecting with them in this way. I found an instructor through a friend of Kate's. She had background and training in EFL work as well, which was a relief to me. I felt more comfortable beginning this next part of my horse journey with someone who knew that horses had the gift of being able to help humans with their personal growth and evolution, because it resonated with the ways I understood and approached horses.

Unfortunately, with riding, I became aware of more of the dark side of horse culture. At one of the ranches where I rode, I saw behavior patterns in horse owners that were similar to behaviors I'd observed at riding centers and rescue organizations. I would hear people make comments about how horses were stupid, how they needed to be controlled or dominated. *Show 'em who's boss* and *give 'em a firm hand* were phrases that lingered over the round pens and riding arenas.

I knew this was the way that many had been taught, and these were the belief systems they maintained. Of course, they didn't see it as being controlling or manipulative of horses. But I viewed it differently; and I knew it firsthand. Like when I began my horsemanship training, I saw a lot of hitting and shoving, especially if a horse didn't do what a human wanted. There were also ideas of "not letting a horse get away with anything" floating in the air. It seemed like they couldn't be cut a break.

I remember a particular riding lesson I happened to witness on my way out of the ranch one afternoon. A woman rode her horse in the arena while her instructor watched. She was training for a show that weekend, and needed to get all of the gaits and timing perfected. The movement of horse and rider seemed to flow together beautifully from what I could see, but every once in awhile the horse would toss her head in the air. The instructor would then call out to her student to rein her horse in more.

This is what the rider did, over and over again. The poor horse was foaming at the mouth and stiffly jerking her head in objection to the tightening of the reins. At one point the instructor told the rider she was letting her horse control the situation, and said it was time for her to take charge. There were forceful, jerking rein movements and in frustration, the rider screamed at her horse to stop. As I watched, I could tell the horse was in pain, and something was off. From the heavy feeling in my gut, I knew that this horse was not trying to dominate anyone. She was simply trying to communicate something to them and they were missing it.

The following week, I overheard two horsewomen standing outside that horse's stall, talking about an emergency visit by the vet that day. Apparently the horse had a tooth that needed to be pulled because the bit rubbed that area of her mouth when she tossed her head, causing pain. It sounded as if this had been happening off and on, unbeknownst to the horse's owner. I kept my eyes on the horse while I listened to the two humans share how bummed they were that the horse didn't get to show last week. This horse had regret and guilt written all over her. She shook her head and slit her eyes in agony, as if to say, "I'm sorry, so sorry." She wanted to cooperate with her human but couldn't, and felt terrible for letting her down.

This is an important example for humans to think about when considering why a horse is misbehaving. He or she might be in pain, and might be trying to communicate that to us. Any human could have easily missed the real reason behind the behavior of this horse, assuming that the horse was being defiant, trying to control the situation, or just plain lazy. This horse's suffering is a lesson for us in being open to ruling out all the potential reasons our horses may not follow our requests.

Don't get me wrong. I am well aware that horses, like dogs, prefer a leader. If you are passive or are not more of a leader than they are, they will take charge in most situations, which means they may do things you may not want them to do. But I have always known in my heart that this leadership can be relayed through energy-based training methods, personal mastery, and the clear communication and connection you have with your horse, not by using force with your body or any tool. I also know that, like the situation I've just described, it is important to keep an open mind, because there might be times where it would be appropriate for a horse to take the lead. Situations can arise where their survival or yours might be threatened. If you were on a trail and your horse sensed real danger ahead, wouldn't you want him to take the initiative and turn around, or at least refuse to move forward until it is safe?

Physical violence not only causes physical pain, but it also causes emotional and mental harm. I have seen the looks on the faces of the horses that get smacked. They feel confused, other times betrayed, or both. I have also seen trainers and equestrians kick their horses while standing before them, explaining in their own defense that it's okay for humans to do this to teach them a lesson because horses do it to each other all the time. With the experience I have since gained working with horses physically and intuitively, I have never found this to be true. Although horses kick each other to set boundaries and assert dominance, if we engage in this kind of behavior with them it often leads to more fights and struggle, not true leadership based on an equal partnership.

We are humans, their natural predators since the beginning of time. Any kind of physical threat we inflict upon them ignites their prey instincts, which creates fear. Fear in turn causes mistrust, and compromises the integrity of our relationship with horses. Even in a dangerous situation, one where our survival or safety is threatened, we always have the option of taking action that doesn't involve violence.

For example, let's say you are grooming your horse and out of nowhere he rears up or kicks out at you in a way that could or does cause injury. I recommend finding out why he reared and kicked out. Was there a loud noise, a flying plastic bag or debris in his field of vision, or is he having a reaction to a physical sensation, a bite or bee sting, or the way you are grooming?

If it's one of these reasons or something similar, the horse is responding instinctually, which is normal behavior in a healthy horse. You don't want to inhibit this internal response by punishing him for it. Dimming these reflexes leads to a horse that becomes dissociated, less active and interactive within his environment, and causes the inability to be fully present, whole, and alive. The best thing we can do as humans is to stay in the present moment at all times when we are with our horses, so we can move to safety quickly and easily if they respond instinctually. Although I would never blame a human for defending himself in a dangerous situation, it's important to remember that if we are choosing to work or play with horses, then we are choosing to take on physical risk due to their large size, fast speed, and instinctual nature.

On the other hand, if you find that the horse in the above example was not acting instinctually—not responding to anything or anyone in their environment, and instead was acting out of an attempt to control, dominate, or refuse to cooperate—I recommend working this issue out with them through ground work and basic horsemanship activities, not force or violence. Find a trainer who can teach you energy-based horsemanship skills and leadership. Practicing these skills clearly and consistently with your horse will help them learn to trust and respect you while maintaining their safety and dignity. You will also deepen the bond with them and gain their cooperation by responding to their body language, like in the examples throughout this book, and using the animal communication and healing tools I provide in Chapter Twelve. As Adele and Marlena McCormick shared in their book *Horse Sense and the Human Heart: What Horses Can Teach Us About Trust, Bonding, Creativity and Spirituality*, "To establish trust with animals, we have to base our interactions on honesty, mutual respect and compassion."[1]

We must keep in mind that many horses have emotional baggage, just as we do, which may involve having been abandoned, abused, or dominated by another human or animal and developing coping mechanisms to avoid or survive a similar circumstance. Sometimes individual horses even act out in response to the emotional trauma held in the horse collective energy field—the trauma carried by all horses through all times. In these rare cases, there will be no logical reason for their inappropriate behavior. Ground work and horsemanship activities, as well as getting them the healing they deserve for both individual and collective trauma, will lead to the best results.

During the time I was beginning to ride, I heard many people talk about wanting to have a good relationship with their horse—wanting there to be respect on both sides. Like all relationships with humans or any other beings, how can we develop respect if there isn't trust? How can we develop trust if we are afraid and don't feel safe? Practicing this new way of relating to them, as well as setting boundaries that create safety for ourselves and the horses, will in turn lead to the cooperation, trust, and respect that we desire.

ANGEL

Desiring a True Friend

The first horse I learned to ride was Angel, a spotted Appaloosa, with swirls of black and white on her barrel that reminded me of the yin-yang symbol. I met a few of the other horses available for me to ride around the same time, but when I was introduced to Angel, she moved in continuous circles in her stall, nickered under her breath, and made eye contact with me the whole time. I knew she was choosing me. So I spent our first two experiences grooming and connecting with her.

Angel lived up to her name. She was sweet, understanding, and loving. She was also an assertive horse. Right off, she had no trouble telling me where she liked to be rubbed and brushed. She had touchy hooves, and by trying to pull away from me and biting at the air, she made it clear that she wasn't a fan of me cleaning them. I felt affection from her in the way she liked to nuzzle my hands or shoulder. It didn't take long for us to bond.

From her current owner, I learned that Angel had been bounced around from owner to owner over the previous ten years. She was a good, solid, steady, and reliable horse, especially on the trails because she knew them well. But she was older, nearing twenty-five, and she had a sore right shoulder and hip, making cantering difficult. Many of her owners would get tired of her after awhile, and sell her for a horse who was able to do more. My heart went out to her.

Like the workshop horses, Angel really taught me what true connection and partnership are about. Through knowing her, I began to understand how sensitive horses really are. Not only can they sense how their riders feel, they can even feel a fly land on their butt! When we consider that level of sensitivity, we can understand the importance in helping horses keep this vital part of their nature intact. Thereafter, it is easier for horses to better know and understand what our intentions are with riding and anything else we are doing together, and our desires can be more easily conveyed to them through our words, body language, energy, and the positioning of body parts such as our lower legs and heels while riding.

When I first started riding, it was a completely new experience and I was afraid. It is risky, similar to driving a car in that the large size and fast speed could lead to injury. But riding horses is different than driving a car because horses have their own individual thoughts, feelings, instincts, and desires. We have even less control when we get on our horse than we do when we get into our car every day. Even though a skilled rider can adjust accordingly when in a dangerous situation, one can never be completely sure how a certain horse will react on a specific day under particular circumstances. Yet, we still yearn for the freedom and joy riding brings. As we are taught by our experiences in all kinds of relationships, there can be so much delight and at the same time we fear getting hurt by what could be an unfortunate turn of events.

From the beginning, when I started to ride her at just a walk and trot in the arena, I always knew Angel would take care of me. She conveyed this easily to me by the way her body would move in the direction of mine when I was off-balance in the saddle, and with her upright, backward ear position that would always focus on me. She was there for me, consistently tuning in to the energy behind my verbal or body commands. If I was fearful of trotting, she would pick up on this and not follow through. Because she was a lead mare, I really had to be assertive when I wanted a particular response. I remember my riding instructor calling out to me one day: "Say it like you mean it!" Angel preferred to trot at a speedy pace. Because her trot felt extra bumpy to me, I had to let her know that I wanted her to slow down. Most of the time she followed through, when my energy matched my words.

There were times I was happy to let her lead. I did this when I went trail riding with her, because it was new and I didn't know the way. Although I went with another experienced rider, I sent Angel the message that I was comfortable letting her take charge of the direction we'd go in, but not the pace. I told her this out loud, as if I was telling another human, and I also sent the thoughts from my mind to hers, using my imagination like I did with the workshop horses. As expected, things went smoothly. Angel deferred to me when it came to slowing down as I gently took in the reins and relaxed my energy. Even in areas where we went up and down steep slopes, my initial anxiety gave way and the rides were a breeze. I learned to let go and trust. Angel was able to pick through the rocky hills gracefully and we moved together harmoniously. After doing this a few times it started to feel familiar and fun, and I always looked forward to it.

With all of our work together, I quickly overcame my original fear of being on a huge, fast-moving, free thinking mammal. I realized how simply getting on the back of a horse for the first time could help one overcome the anxiety that comes with the unknown in any area of life. After several months I was moving at a fast trot in the arena, changing directions and leads, backing up, doing figure eights around barrels, and riding the trails regularly.

One day after a long trail ride, I spent some extra time with Angel outside her stall. I could always tell she appreciated extra nurturing and care by the way she lowered her head, and relaxed her eyes and face. I usually gave her a deep massage with her groom, combed her mane and tail, and put some shiny conditioner in them for a sleek look and feel. I often joked with the other horse people that she was the spa horse of the ranch.

This time, I felt something unexpected coming from Angel when I finished. There was a tenderness in her presence. I tuned in like I did with the workshop horses, and in my psychic vision I saw a pink line of energy going from her heart to mine. I sent this loving energy back to her, and told her how thankful I was for having her in my life. As I opened myself up to her further, I felt the vulnerability in her question: "Now that you trust me, can I trust you?"

Taking her need to heart, I took a deep breath. I wanted to make sure I understood. She continued, "I have had many people in my life. I have kids that ride me regularly and the enjoyment is equally shared. But I yearn for someone who wishes to remain in my life forever. A true friend." I stood back and stared at the ground. I didn't know what to tell her. How could I guarantee I would always be in her life? She was only the first horse I had ridden, and I didn't own her. I didn't live in the same town she was in, and with the way my life was changing I had no idea where I would be in a year.

I realized that Angel was being open and honest with me. I knew that she was looking for genuineness and intimacy with a human. I watched her around other horses, and although she definitely shared the bond of the herd, she lit up around her human companions. So I told her the truth. I could be in her life right now, but I had no idea how long that would be because of all the changes I was going through. I asked her if she would be okay with that as I held my breath. She grimaced, as if I had just slapped her, and stared back, dumbfounded. I reminded her that I truly loved her, and that we could celebrate this closeness in our relationship for however long it would be.

When I left that night I knew I did the right thing, but I couldn't help feeling remorseful about letting Angel down. I knew that the longing Angel had for a forever human in her life was more than likely shared by many other animals as well. At least, perhaps for the first time, she would have a human in her life that would not pretend or make false promises. Although she didn't know how long our relationship would last, she knew I was reliable, honest, and nurturing when we were together. Similar to humans, it was also a lesson for her about loss because we never really know how long someone will be in our lives. We will all eventually leave our loved ones through death, if not before due to other circumstances. What we can take away from grief is the wisdom that we are always connected to the essence of what that human or animal meant to us. We carry this inside of us for eternity. This is the basis behind the old saying, "True love never dies."

COMANCHE
Deserving Consideration and Commitment

Time went on at the ranch where I rode Angel, and I had more to learn. Sometimes I watched the kids ride, because they seemed to enjoy it even more than adults. It was their joy and play, not necessarily about the seriousness of technique or competition. One of the boys, David, was riding a horse named Comanche, a gorgeous, sixteen-hand bay Thoroughbred, with warm, gentle, chocolate-colored eyes.

David told me Comanche had been a polo horse for ten years, but severely injured his leg, which led to an automatic retirement. Now he was owned by one of the local riding instructors. I remembered overhearing some other horse people say he was a solid, steady horse who never spooked or bolted. So he was great for working with kids. I could see that Comanche liked his new line of work. There was an excitement that sparkled in his eyes when David approached, and a lightness in his step when they rode together. I was glad for this, because I noticed that he seemed to go to a dreadful place later, after David would leave for the day. The brightness left his eyes, and his head hung low, sulkily. Sadness seemed to emanate from him. It was like the difference between night and day, literally like the flip of a switch.

I stood outside his stall during one of his moods. I wanted to see what all this mournfulness was about. Just then, a picture passed before my eyes. I saw a rider on him, pushing him forward with his willful energy and body. Comanche looked tired and tense. I sensed a great deal of pressure. Other pictures flooded my vision. I saw many workouts and strict routines. The rider was always looking at his watch and Comanche was always working and sweating. I felt feelings of not being good enough and fear of failure. Then there was stomach pain and anxiety. What a life!

I asked Comanche if this is what bothered him so much when everyone went home for the day. Is this what he thought about during his free time? He sent me feelings of grief and regret. I saw a picture of the rider's face again. After a few more exchanges of energy, I came to the conclusion that the polo life was stressful for Comanche, and he didn't miss it as much as he did his former human. He also thought he had screwed up in some way. From what I could tell, he blamed himself for losing some of the matches and getting hurt. I asked him what happened when he got injured. He sent me fear and sadness, and showed me an angry rider. I was overcome with heartache as I empathized with Comanche. He had been abandoned by the one he loved the most.

I began to reflect on what we did to horses. We were dedicated and devoted to them in companionship, competition, and work, but if they got hurt or could no longer do the same thing they had been doing we often traded them in like an old, worn-out Mercedes. What kind of relationship was that? They were fully committed to being our partners, but where was our commitment to them?

In the case of Comanche, something inside of me seemed to reveal that less pressure and a lighter work routine could have potentially prevented the injury. I wondered if his human ever considered how this lifestyle affected his horse. Did he even care how Comanche felt during all of these activities and the need to be the best, which was evident in his fear of failing? Or was it all about what he, the owner, wanted?

I was starting to think that we were treating horses as objects—continuing to do whatever we wanted with them, to their detriment. This was no way to show gratitude for their lifelong loyalty to service and friendship. Maybe this was a pattern that got passed down through our ancestors, without ever being reconsidered. Centuries ago, we needed horses to survive. They took us to war and worked in our fields. Today that is not the case. I knew from my experience volunteering and riding that horses wanted to be partners in our lives, in a way that was mutually beneficial. When were we going to change how we related to and cared for these benevolent beings?

This outrage continued to pulsate in my mind in the days that followed. The documentary *The Path of the Horse: Taking The First Step*,[2] was recommended to me by my riding instructor and some horse colleagues. In the film, many horse professionals discuss the new role horses play in the lives of humans, one that fits the purpose of our relationship with them in this current time. They talk about true partnership, treating horses as equals, which means recognizing that they have as much to teach us as we do them. One of the biggest themes in the documentary is that we can still ride for competition or fun, but it is time to do it in a way that supports the horse's health. Some horses who were part of the research for the film had x-rays of their backs, showing injuries that would be called abuse if seen in humans.

From what I could understand from the film, the humans who owned these horses were not doing anything outrageous when they were riding. This led me to believe that we could be hurting our horses and not even know it. They might not even complain or act like they are in pain, often because they become so used to it. In other cases, horses keep quiet because of their dedication to service—the desire to please us. The documentary makes a point of educating us on how to prevent this. Some of the professionals mentioned the importance of making sure a saddle fits well if we can't ride bareback, avoiding spurs, and using less severe bits or bitless bridles whenever possible.

I cringed when I thought of my riding experience with Angel. At times in the beginning, I reined her in quick and hard to slow down or change direction. I also occasionally yanked on the reins to get her to stop. It had been a combination of fear and wanting things to go my way, but now I wondered how that had been for her. It made me feel better at the time to think that maybe she was used to it. Perhaps after years of riding, especially carrying all those kids, it didn't bother her as much anymore. I also knew many horses were handled much more harshly in training methods where they were "broke."

I never questioned how she felt until now. I contemplated how Angel thought of me as her friend. Adele, Marlena, and Thomas McCormick stated in their book *Horses and the Mystical Path: The Celtic Way of Expanding the Human Soul*, with horses, "Friendship is about giving and receiving,"[3] and each benefitting from the relationship. I thought of a friend as an ally and a support, not someone who received without consideration for someone else's feelings. I knew it was time to repay the debt, but I didn't yet know how.

Soon after viewing this documentary, I ran into Comanche's current human. Her name was Diane and she was an experienced horsewoman. She grew up riding and had trained and taught for the past twenty years. I heard through other horse people that she was open to many of the new ideas about EFL work, and how we could interact with horses without dominating them. She happened to share with me that Comanche also came with some very heavy-duty back injuries from his former polo days. It didn't surprise me. I mentioned the documentary *The Path of the Horse*, thinking she had probably not seen it but might be interested in it.

I was amazed and disappointed by her incredulity. She had seen it but did not appreciate the ideas in it. Like the common tone I seemed to be picking up that consisted of repeating the same, familiar, outdated methods in training and riding, Diane didn't think change was necessary. Her theory seemed to be that even if there were documented injuries from everyday riding, horses have always functioned and provided for us without difficulty. So why should we bother with change? She expressed that Comanche's situation was different. He was pushed to his limit and polo was a completely different lifestyle, much like a professional football player's is, compared to someone who plays football for fun.

But I thought she was contradicting herself. Does it really make no difference what we are doing with our horses, if it is injuring or harming them in any way? Whether they let us know or not, shouldn't we care enough to become more conscientious? The irritated defensiveness that permeated Diane's and many horse people's explanations for their actions and interactions with their horses scared me. This conversation was not about one person's opinion. It was the opinion of many. Are we ignoring the truth because we are afraid of change, or is it simply our own stubborn refusal to give up having our cake and eating it at the expense of our horses? I also wondered why Diane and other horse people would get angry or defensive at all. This was about exploring other options for improving our horses' health and happiness, and our relationship with them, not making anyone right or wrong in the matter.

Perhaps this defensiveness stemmed from the collective human guilt for our mistreatment of horses over hundreds of years. Horses had been beasts of burden. Many wore their bodies down in war, farming, and cross country travel, and were forced to press on even when they couldn't keep up the work. But times have changed. We must face the feelings about our actions in the past, so we can move on, and do what is best for our horses now.

As the conversation with Diane echoed in my mind on the drive home that day, I decided it was time to get the training in EFL. I felt more prepared emotionally and intellectually, now having participated in additional workshops and individual EFL sessions that year.

I also noticed a shift in my intention. It wasn't just about learning an innovative modality to help humans heal. It was now about my passion to serve horses. I wanted to understand, connect, and communicate with them on a deeper level, so I could be one of the humans out there who truly wanted to give back. I knew this was part of my calling; I knew this was why the horses had cried out to me in my dreams. They wanted change in their human relations. Because of this fervent passion that ignited in me while learning to ride, I could no longer deny my destiny.

CHAPTER FOUR

HORSES' MEDICINE

I finally received my training in Equine Facilitated Mental Health (EFMH), which is similar to EFL, in Canada. This training focused on EFL work that takes place on the ground, the only kind of work I wanted to facilitate. I enjoyed the training and learned so much, but one thing became very clear to me while I completed it. I would need even more experience before becoming a practitioner of EFL.

The following year an opportunity came up for me to volunteer at a healing workshop. I would mainly be the horse handler, but would also have the chance to facilitate a couple sessions under the guidance of the lead facilitator. It was to take place in none other than Norfolk County, England. I intuitively felt this was the place Kate's horses had been talking about two years before. I also had a dream that gave me the name of the lead facilitator, Brenda Mennings, who was from Cambridge but was hosting the workshop in a rural area of Norfolk. Brenda taught psychology at a secondary school, and like me, had a master's degree in psychology.

After a short interview over the phone, I knew it felt right. I was happy to hear that this workshop operated on the foundations of psychological belief systems that emphasize the importance of safety. Brenda encouraged me to use the workshop opportunity to practice and master my skills in becoming aware of how both horse and human are processing sensory input—the physical, mental/emotional, and energetic stimulation in their environment.

To expand upon this further, it is the role of the EFL facilitator to make adjustments as needed for both parties. During a professional training called Reflection of the Horse, taught by Deborah Marshall, Advanced Epona Instructor and Equine Facilitated Mental Health practitioner, I discovered that, if a human or horse is getting over-stimulated, you can decrease the amount of sensory input by decreasing or eliminating activities. A human or horse who is getting disoriented or ungrounded through the intensity experienced while in the presence of the other's energy, or with the emotions that arise because of the closeness, might be taken out of the round pen or given the physical space needed to reground and center.

In cases of too little stimulation, or where one is bored or checking out, an increase in sensory input can help them become more alert, focused, and aware of their body and surroundings. One way to do this is to "slow things down." Have the human or horse engage in a simple physical activity like walking, grooming, eating, or "noticing the sensations in the environment around them—feeling the wind blow their hair, the sun on their face, or the smells of the flowers and trees."[1]

I learned in a previous workshop called Horses As Mirrors of Our Souls, taught by Eve Lee, Advanced Epona Instructor and shamanic practitioner, that without being fully present, the magical, alchemical process of healing cannot occur.[2] Both horse and human need to be in the present moment for the experience of feeling, knowing, and sensing what is happening inside of them, on a body, mind, and spirit level.

Because of my background in psychology, I understood the need for safe space, a container to allow one to process their emotions, the physical happenings, and the energy in the environment in a balanced way. From what I experienced in all the EFL workshops I had attended over the previous year, I learned that the container consists of the human, the horse, the facilitator of the session, and the round pen or place where the session takes place. The facilitator's role in holding safe space is to be consciously aware of what's happening with the horse and human, making sure that both parties remain grounded and in the present moment, able to actively experience their emotions. A facilitator's compassion, in addition to a heightened awareness and presence, helps bring forth a profound level of healing and transformation for horse and human during an EFL session.

From my studies in counseling psychology, I knew that ensuring safety is always the first step needed to begin healing. Without it, a person would have to use his energy for protection, not healing or transformation. I realized this idea applied just the same to horses and humans participating in EFL. In addition, what I took from Marshall's training was that a lack of safety in the case of an unnoticed over- or under-stimulating situation could be dangerous, leading to accidents or injuries, diminished or less meaningful interactions between horse and human, or either horse or human becoming so flooded with emotion that being able to ground and function normally in their environment would become nearly impossible.

What Brenda and I discussed in the phone interview reminded me of the experiences I had while working at one of California's Therapeutic Riding Academies (TRA). There were many physically or mentally handicapped children who rode the horses there. Some were autistic or had Down syndrome; others were labeled with Attention Deficit Hyperactivity Disorder (ADHD). I was always amazed at the changes I noticed in these children after riding, and how this benefitted the horses as well.

CHILDREN AND HORSES
Mutual Alchemy

One boy is prominent in my memory for the healing he experienced with a beautiful Paint gelding named Freckles. The boy, Jack, was given the diagnosis of autism at the age of four. While I was at the TRA, he was seven years old and still could not speak full sentences and had frequent temper tantrums that alternated with periods of time where he zoned or spaced out. He had many sleepless nights, often pacing the upstairs hall for hours. When his parents came upon him in the middle of the night, what they thought they understood from his few simple words was that he was only trying to feel his feet.

Freckles was a horse that most were beginning to give up on. He had previously been a happy-go-lucky trail and ranch horse who belonged to only one human most of his life. When he reached an old age, having difficulty with fast-paced, longer riding and ranch work due to sore hips and joints, his human gave him to the TRA, thinking he would be able to handle lower intensity riding, as well as enjoy the kids. Unfortunately, the opposite was occurring. Since being with the TRA, Freckles was becoming withdrawn, spending large portions of time tucked away in his paddock, with his head sagging low. He would not go out to greet the other horses head-to-head over the fences, and he would not come to any human who entered his paddock, with or without a halter. He was also eating very little. The staff and volunteers were perplexed as to how to handle the situation.

A month went by, with little change. They were considering giving him back to his human, because he still would not work with anyone at the facility. In fact, if someone did get close to approaching him, he would flatten his ears and flare his nostrils, quickly retreating to his private space out of sight. If he did not soon improve, there would be no place for him there.

Then Jack showed up. From the first moment he eyed Freckles over the fence, the staff noticed a change in the energy of this horse. That first day, Freckles peeked his head out from behind the covered paddock. In just a couple weeks, he was meeting Jack at the gate regularly, sniffing him, quietly nickering, and giving his full, front-facing-eared attention. They started off touching each other and grooming in Freckles' paddock. It was amazing to see the horse's interest and fondness of Jack. His eyes lightened and he even wagged his tail like a dog while pointing with his muzzle to show Jack exactly where he wanted to be rubbed.

It wasn't long, perhaps a couple weeks, before they were riding together. They began at a walk, and then easily flowed into a soft trot. Jack would arrive some days aloof, and other times anxious and irritable. When they rode, an instant change was visible. If he seemed off in a faraway world, Jack would quickly become grounded and present when he picked up the reins and directed Freckles. He would even speak sentences on these particular rides, grabbing Freckles' mane and telling him to go faster, turn down a certain path on a trail, or look at a bunny that crossed the path. Of course, Freckles missed nothing, and Jack would have to bring his focus back to the road and not the animals on it, or they would find themselves going in a completely different direction. Jack made these adjustments look easy, unlike at home, where his parents struggled to get him to stay focused on simply eating a meal.

One day Jack was at his worst. His parents reported that he had temper tantrums and refused to do any activities or speak to anyone all day. Mostly he just screamed and pounded his fists. When he arrived at the TRA, he was red-faced, solemn, edgy, and appeared on the verge of another outburst. One of the volunteers brought Freckles out to him right away. As soon as he got up in the saddle, Jack let out a blood-curdling screech, leaned forward and slapped both sides of Freckles' neck. The TRA staff and I stood there holding our breath. Freckles stood as still as a statue. We looked at each other in disbelief, mouths gaping open, while the shouting continued for about thirty more seconds. Freckles remained a completely calm, motionless horse.

Then Jack told him to walk on. Freckles took off at an even pace, carrying Jack with the usual grace and dignity that came to be discovered as his true nature. Two volunteers and I flanked both of his sides. We watched as Jack breathed slowly and deeply in complete rhythm with Freckles' movements. He was grasping the reins, looking straight ahead. They moved together harmoniously, as if they were one body.

Jack's riding instructor decided to teach him to canter in this lesson, because he was doing so well. During their trot Jack began laughing and shouting out, this time with glee, and he seemed more intently aware, unlike any other previous lesson. When he asked Freckles to canter, they took off more briskly, with a soothing, rocking-chair motion. As they glided along, we were captivated. When it came time to stop, the riding lesson ended with peace and calm. Unlike when he first arrived, Jack gave Freckles a big hug and with a smile, skipped over to his mother who was waiting by the sidelines.

After I left the TRA, I found out that Jack continued to ride Freckles every week for another year or so. His temper tantrums diminished to rare occasions, he was more grounded and present in his everyday activities, and was speaking more fluently. His parents were so impressed they even bought him his own pony, so he could ride on a daily basis. It was an awesome healing process, based on balancing the sensory stimulation through vacillating amounts of touch and movement. Jack was able to moderate this with Freckles as his grounding rod.

Freckles seemed to heal as well. He became alive, alert, and back to his original cheerful nature. I learned that Freckles remained upbeat and accommodating, even when Jack wasn't around. He was willing to work every day, now meeting every child or adult who came into his paddock.

This positive outcome inspired me to discover more about how horses and kids together formed a mutually beneficial relationship. With the time I spent at the TRA and from some of the riding instructors I met at the ranch where I rode Angel, I learned how much healing resulted from interactions between horses and children, whether in the saddle or on the ground.

Through having to be aware of the task at hand, children can be helped to focus better, and are easily grounded and centered by horses. This is especially true for highly sensitive, gifted children, as well as those like Jack, with the conditions and diagnoses mentioned earlier. While seated on a horse or standing next to them, it is easy for their energy to be exchanged. Empathic children are able to release the energies they have been picking up from their family members, playmates, and the world through everyday activities spent with the horses. As they release these heavy emotions and physical sensations, they feel lighter, more relaxed and calm.

Horses also help kids stay healthy through their strong, grounded presence, and unconditional love. There is no judgment in horses, like there is with many adult humans. You don't have to explain this intellectually to a kid. They know unconsciously if someone has the inner strength to support them through their life challenges as well as if someone really gets them. Horses can do both. Even horses who carry trauma related to living an emotionally or physically challenging life can help a child who has experienced similar life circumstances.

This is because of what Linda Kohanov described in *The Tao of Equus* as a similar resonance in their energy field. The resonance could be on an emotional, physical, or mental level, meaning they have common health issues, emotional tendencies, and patterns of thought. In either case, the horse and child will be comfortable in each other's presence. The relationship will feel familiar, like meeting an old friend. Being at ease with one another helps form the bond needed to begin the healing process. On top of that, a horse's genuine expression makes it easier for kids to relate to their own emotions, and it also supports them in accepting who they are innately—their own uniqueness.

All children can benefit from spending any amount of time with horses, irrespective of whether they are considered gifted, disabled, or sensitive. These are the labels of our culture, which miss the magnificence of each human's precious soul. Every child is special—and horses, being the psychic, empathic animals that they are, know their talents and strengths, helping to draw them out and expand them. From what I had observed at the TRA, horses help provide balance in a child's body, personality, or spirit. If a child is more left-brained, logical, or rational, the horses will offer them the chance to delve into the world of imagination, intuition, and creativity.

I have talked to kids who reported, after riding or spending time with horses, increased or budding psychic abilities, such as seeing auras, knowing their spirit guides, having a deeper interest in art or music, and even being aware of having healing abilities. I once met a mother who reported that her son Joey, who was introduced to horses through a neighbor, was previously a timid, quiet, isolated child, and was often depressed. She had been worried about his social skills and emotional stability. After a few afternoons interacting with the horses, Joey already appeared to be enjoying life more. He excitedly shared conversations he had with the horses, and was putting his hands on the dogs at home, saying he was helping them feel better. He was also opening up to other kids at school, making friendships based on his new passion with animals.

Many kids I worked with who were highly emotional and sensitive, right-brained, and over-stimulated by life, like Freckles' friend Jack, received the opposite benefit: a deepening of their left-brained faculties, groundedness, and better control of and presence in their physical bodies. As Adele and Marlena McCormick wrote in *Horse Sense and the Human Heart*, "Finding a rhythm, whether in the saddle or running beside a horse, gives us a sense of being rocked or cradled. Rhythmic movement facilitates growth in premature babies and soothes fussy infants."[3] This rhythmic rocking of a horse in motion can calm and reset any overactive neurological system.

I have seen blind children compensate by developing better-than-average hearing; I have heard of paraplegics who developed such increased upper body strength they are able to get themselves around almost as much as they would have with legs that worked effectively. In the two examples of the handicapped above, these changes happened over the course of several years. But nonetheless, in all the cases, including Jack's, it is incredible to see these results, all because of the regular practice of basic horsemanship—grooming, haltering, leading, riding, and dance and art therapy with the horses.

The horses enjoy their time with kids, too. Many of them light up when the kids come around. Children tend to maintain their true nature until they reach the teenage years or older. My professional experience in both nursing and counseling has shown me that in our busy, fast-paced, success-oriented world, by the time they reach puberty a child's individual soul spark can be drowned out by the pressure of life events, responsibilities, and the influence of authority figures who have rigid ideas about who they are and what they are expected to do and be. Horses are attracted to the joy, wonder, and innocence that are inherent in young children. It is like a breath of fresh air when compared to many jaded, cynical adults.

Horses can also relate to the overemphasized nonverbal cues and body language that are often seen in many sensitive or disabled children. They take pleasure in nurturing and healing these children. Similar to the workshop horses, I noticed that even those horses at the TRA who were hardened by life seemed to want to help kids heal. Except for the few horses who were ill or nearing retirement and unable, I never met a horse there who seemed unwilling to work with the kids. In fact, in cases like Freckles' I found that some of the horses healed and changed for the better, as much as the children did.

THE WORKSHOP

Sensing Safely and the Right Use of Power

After the interview with Brenda, having time to reflect on the need for safety and presence and how that benefitted both horse and human, I decided to make the trip to England for the workshop. The process of getting there was a bumpy one, but not from the actual flight. I was already feeling like a stranger in a strange land; the paperwork and security checkpoints seemed endless and exhausting.

While at the arrival gate in the Norwich Airport I experienced a shocking and anxious interaction with a ticket agent and subsequent security official. They were checking our boarding passes and passports when I got off the plane because of increased security measures. Something seemed to be wrong with my boarding pass or passport. The ticket agent took me to a security official, who looked everything over extensively.

I went through a long process of having to explain and confirm my identity, current residence, and where I purchased my original ticket. When I checked in at the U.S. airport, I was whisked through without a problem. But now Norwich security checked my passport and their computers for additional verification. I waited in nervous anticipation. I wasn't sure what was wrong or why I was being detained.

Was there something out there blocking me from attending this important workshop? I certainly began to wonder. But then somehow it all got cleared up. I don't even remember exactly how it happened. I know that I felt a strong burst of support coming from around the center of my body. The airport security official eventually looked up at me and told me to head on through and to enjoy my time in Norwich.

Looking back, I now think that, without my knowing it, the magic of my own power dissolved the complication. It could have been my guides, although at the time I didn't know much about the helper guides in the spirit world.

This unusual airport experience was a precursor for what I was in for during the workshop. The humble beginnings of the awareness of my own power became more obvious to me throughout it. From the first day on, the workshop was not just teaching me how to be with horses, it was teaching me how to be with people.

This workshop consisted of a group of ten people, including many healing professionals and some interested in becoming facilitators of this work. When I had my chance to facilitate a couple sessions, I worked with two people who struggled with their own personal blocks to healing. I realized it was partly due to the fact that many of us were colleagues who wanted to maintain a certain professional demeanor with each other. Because of this, I could understand why some of the participants were not willing to open up fully to the horses and facilitators in the sessions.

But it was also slightly bewildering to me, as I was there—and so assumed others were as well—because I was determined to discover more about myself and how I could grow, so I could move forward in my work. No matter how vulnerable or exposed I could potentially feel in these sessions, I had not forgotten my intentions from working with the horses in New Jersey. And with the horses, it was always a fun process. But not everyone saw it the same way I did.

The first student I worked with, Jill, said that all she wanted to do was groom the mysterious black gelding she was drawn to in the barn, and then walk him out into the pasture. I agreed she could do the session in the barn with the horse called Jade, but I told her that I would need to see how things flowed in each moment, before deciding about the pasture. As we checked in together before starting the session, I noticed Jill was turning away from my energy and didn't appear to be doing the exercises to get grounded, present, and prepared to be with the horse.

When Jill went into the barn and Jade's stall, although she was spending time with him, attempting to touch and groom him, she was not truly participating, only going through the motions. I was watching from the front door of the barn. Jill wasn't focused on what was happening inside of herself. My clue was Jade's behavior. He moved to the back of his stall in the barn several times in the beginning and would not engage with her. I heard him tell me over and over that she was not being genuine, which was essential for the session to be a benefit to her. As I had learned in previous horse workshops, you must be present with your innermost life to receive the shift you desire on an emotional, mental, physical, or spiritual level.

Up until this point in the session, I had temporarily stepped down in my power, deferring to another's agenda like I had often done in my personal life.

Since I was still a novice in facilitating EFL sessions, I cut myself some slack. But I was also very aware of what was going on and decided to change old patterns from the past by doing something different in the now. Jill's resistance to be real with herself is what Linda Kohanov described as "incongruence" in *Riding Between the Worlds*: the unconscious, masking of emotions through a physical façade.[4] I was relieved to see that despite this fact, Jade was keeping Jill safe through his distance. This is very important in EFL sessions, because horses are large animals. If the person is not actively aware of or processing their emotions, the animal could act out the hidden, chaotic energy in an unpredictable way, leading to accidents.

I asked Jill to step out of the barn, so we could wrap up the session from the outside. We discussed what went on between her and the horse, and how she felt throughout the session. I emphasized what Wyatt Webb said in his book *It's Not About the Horse: It's About Overcoming Fear and Self Doubt*: "Authenticity is the key to connection with horses."[5] As Adele and Marlena McCormick shared in *Horse Sense and the Human Heart,* horses respond to what is going on inside of us, helping us to access our inner creativity and innate healing source. The McCormicks go on to say that horses "can touch deep recesses in us that are inaccessible to most people—regions people are afraid to address in others, much less themselves."[6]

For some people this can feel threatening or overwhelming, while for others it can be exhilarating. I asked Jill if any of these emotions came up while in Jade's presence. Jill told me she felt neither overwhelmed nor excited during the session but that she would reflect on what we had discussed, which would help her process the information and experience, perhaps becoming more aware of what went on in the session. I reminded her that there would be more time available during the weekend to discuss anything about the session that might come into her awareness later.

A similar issue came up with another student. Although Rose was easily able to get grounded and be present, when she walked into the round pen I felt enormous fear come up in me. Panicking inwardly, I watched as the towering, chocolate-colored Thoroughbred sped up and circled the round pen in a whirlwind. I knew I had not been nervous before, so I questioned whether I was picking up on Rose's energy. I had recently started understanding the extent of my empathic abilities from receiving an energy session with a Qigong Master. My energy fields absorbed much more in my physical environment than I was frequently aware of. As I watched the quick, edgy movements of the horse, I discerned that the fear I was feeling was Rose's fear, mirrored in the horse's behavior.

I worked to get Rose focused on what was going on inside, asking her to feel what was happening in her body, to find the place where the fear originated. She told me she felt fluttering in her solar plexus and was breathing with it, but the horse continued to briskly circle and jig-jag around the round pen. Rose expressed that a company she worked at for over ten years had let her go two weeks previously. She didn't know what she was going to do.

Although Rose remained grounded and stayed aware of the sensation in her solar plexus, she continued to restrain herself emotionally. If she hadn't told me about her work situation, it would be impossible to tell from her outer appearance that she had any fear. The horse never slowed down, but appeared actively focused on the task at hand, helping Rose work her energy. To my surprise, near the end of the session a blast of energy that felt like a power surge went through me again, at the level of my solar plexus, and both horse and human calmed. Rose finished the session on a relaxed note, suddenly looking refreshed by the whole experience.

I learned a great deal from facilitating both of these sessions, including discovering the hidden talent and potential I had for success in this type of work. It was time for speaking my truth and not faltering in it—trusting it completely. These experiences were teaching me how to move into a greater level of empowerment, which seemed to save the day whenever I was in trouble lately, even in the subtlest ways.

I had always known that I was surrounded by powerful energy, and that at times, without knowing it, it would move through me to help myself or others, like at the Norwich airport and in Rose's session. But I had no idea yet that I was filled with catalytic energy. Catalytic energy ignites change in others. Throughout my life, people felt this activating force while in my presence. If they were hesitant to make a shift, they would often avoid being around it.

It was a pattern I had developed since I started my healing journey. I thought up until this point that I had lost friends because I was growing out of them due to the speed of my transformational process. This was partly true, but it was also because we would come head-to-head with an issue that needed resolving. Underlying the hashing out of whatever issue we had was the fact that I was using another of my unknown spiritual gifts— being able to pick up on a person's shadow and mirror it to them.

As David Richo explained in *Shadow Dance: Liberating the Power and Creativity of Your Dark Side*, the shadow is the unacknowledged and often repressed negative or positive aspects of oneself. Because I hadn't fully owned my gift yet, I would unknowingly blurt out a word or act out a dynamic that would often trigger the other person. This trigger was their signal to look at what was previously unknown to them. As I gained more awareness about my gift, I would try talking to the other person about what I was intuitively beginning to sense and know. I did this because I truly wanted to have healthy and authentic relationships with others. If they were dishonest, untrustworthy, disrespectful, disloyal, or distant, I would confront it, thinking it was something that could be changed or worked through.

But, as I was slowly figuring out in this frequently lonely journey of spiritual growth, most people did not want to face their core issues. I thought this was because some of the friends I had up until then were not interested in evolving their consciousness. Unfortunately, I even found this true in the counseling world. When I would confront whatever shadow aspect reared up out of the depths, it would often get turned back on me. Of course, I had my own shadow to look at. Even still, I would often be surprised when I would talk about something I wanted to do differently in the relationship. There would frequently be a defensive battle to keep things the way they were.

Fortunately, as I began to consciously own and continue to develop the depth of my gift to see through others and reflect to them their issues, I could immediately tap into what another's capacity is to be in a balanced and earnest relationship, whether with a friend, colleague, business partner, or romantic partner. Now I can make a decision about how to be in relationship with them, if at all.

Similar to what I learned in my personal life, the horse workshop taught me how to use my gifts and power for the best possible outcome in professional relationships with those who would be my future clients. While having the ability to see and trust the truth of each EFL session and each individual's life issues, I developed a higher level of discernment for what each person was ready to discover and process, and was able to adjust the sessions accordingly. I could decide how much contact they would have with a horse, based on their level of awareness, as well as the strength they possessed to integrate new and sometimes disturbing information about the hidden aspects of themselves.

The horse workshop also taught me that horses could help in this process of discernment. Jill and Rose's sessions, as well as the few others that I assisted with in this workshop, revealed this to me: that horses have an uncanny ability to sense how far and deep a person could go during each moment of every session, and would take each person to the edge of their limits. The key to safe, effective healing in this line of work is the support system that the human facilitator or another competent, pre-designated healing professional can provide during the session, immediately afterwards, and up to several months after the session takes place. The purpose of this support system is to provide a safe space to help the client process and integrate the new awareness and healing, while remaining grounded and fully functional in their life.

MARTIE AND BLUE
Spiritual Connection and Family Ties

When it comes to a horse's ability to pierce our illusions and determine our readiness to partake in their revelations, I realized it is their horse-human relationships that help them develop this skill. One example of this involved a horse called Martie. Martie was a sixteen-hand bay Mustang. I was drawn to her from the moment I laid eyes on her. I admired that she was smart, frisky, and feisty, some qualities that I shared with her as well. A couple of people who worked at the ranch where the workshop was held told me about her background. She was abused by an old-fashioned horseman who rode her to a pulp. Bony thin and depressed, Martie was covered in whip marks and spur imprints when she was given away to the human who eventually brought her to the healing ranch where she now lived.

Her new human, Lady, nursed her back to health. She did not even ride Martie for months. She gave her plenty of space, food, love, and nurturing over time. Especially with horses abused under saddle, this freedom from riding is paramount. Lady spent time just being with Martie; they hung out together in the pasture, like a kind of horse teatime. Lady spent an hour or two each day grooming her or walking her in the fields.

She also didn't rush into introducing Martie to the other horses on her property, so it wouldn't be too much pressure for her to fit in all at once. During this time, Martie learned that she didn't really have to do anything, she could just be. Lady thought that Martie must have had a humane human in her life at one time because she healed so quickly. She filled out physically, and became more cheerful, socializing with the horses and humans around her in just a few weeks.

When I started interacting with Martie, I saw a column of white light with my second sight, entering near the crown of her head. I instantly knew that she had a direct connection to the divine, where it entered through her seventh chakra. The white light made me think of unicorns, who have large, spiraling horns projecting from their foreheads, and how they have long been considered spiritual, mythical creatures. I sensed that Martie's spiritual development unfolded because of her relationship with Lady and her new lifestyle. Martie no longer had to do what humans wanted her to do, providing a service and performing a role that was entirely man-made. If she was allowed many hours in the pasture to run free and connect to Earth, with the comfort of food provided and all her needs met, she would not only be able to heal her past, but also unite with the divine in the process.

Return of the spiritual connection in horses is something humankind could work towards in assisting with horses' well-being, even while they carry out many domestic tasks. Horses as a collective struggle with this, as they have so long been our laborers, working for us in the mundane, physical world. Many of them, like humans, lack the awareness of their true identity, of the divine light that runs through them. Instead, they associate their identity with what they do, where they have lived, or who their humans are.

I loved hearing about Martie's success. After spending a few years with Lady, she began working with rehabilitated criminal youth. I was told that Martie shined in this line of work, and seemed to enjoy every minute of it. The ranch workers believed she was able to help these kids because she resonated with what they'd been through due to her own difficult life. Depending on how much Martie had healed and learned to trust again with Lady, it might be less likely that she'd be re-traumatized or reactive to the kids' emotions or behaviors. The kids were also less likely to be triggered by her emotional or physical reactivity, which can open up old wounds.

Because she was an abused horse in the past, Martie might still carry the emotions from the original trauma, which the kids may respond to if they've shared similar experiences. We don't always know the complete history of the horses and humans who come together in this work. But even if a horse or human is re-traumatized, perhaps once again feeling rejected, pushed around, or experiencing fear or dissociation in each other's presence, it gives them the opportunity to finally heal the original wound. As one of my wise healing colleagues once told me, "Sometimes you need a breakdown to have a breakthrough."

This situation would need to be handled delicately, with the help of a competent EFL facilitator who can see and feel what is happening between the horse and human, and will intervene immediately. The EFL facilitator would assist horse and human in working through the trauma in a safe and grounded way, helping them adequately process their emotions without becoming so overwhelmed that staying present and aware would be impossible, and physical reactivity (in the form of unexpected behaviors) could occur. The situation might require that a boundary be set or indicate that a temporary separation is needed. As the healing occurs in this safe setting, and the horse and human shift their energy, the session can end with a feeling, interaction, or behavior dynamic that is different from the past, possibly one never experienced before by either species.

From what the ranch workers told me, it sounded as though Martie had healed substantially and moved into empowerment. She radiated abundant love and compassion, part of which was likely a result of her transformation. I could see why the kids would feel accepted, acknowledged, and completely at ease in the presence of her beautiful energy, thus igniting their healing process.

In addition, because these kids had more than likely been hurt in the past by humans, not horses, they could more easily trust and feel safe with Martie, unlike any human therapist. Regardless of the amount of emotional or physical trauma any animal has experienced, animals in general are still more compassionate than humans. They aren't wired cognitively to judge the way humans do, which is a testament to their healing abilities.

Martie's compassionate and genuine nature brought these kids to the borders of their deepest wounds—helping them face what they needed to about themselves and their lives. Those that observed Martie in her work told me that even the hardest of hearts were softened. Many of these tough, emotionally armored youth would finally let go and cry, embrace Martie, and express gratitude for the experience of knowing her. If they weren't ready to deal with the pain, she would either disengage and head to the opposite side of the round pen, letting them think about it—or begin gently reflecting their suppressed emotions back to them through her body language.

Because of her vivacious energy and charm, I was curious to know more about Martie. I opened up and connected with her, and what came in next amazed me. She started to communicate with me right away. I heard the words in my head: "I want what you want. I am looking for my mate, too." She spun around in the small round pen and raised her head, looking off in all directions. It was as if she was telling me with her body that "he" was out there somewhere. Through her mind again, she asked, "Do you want to know what the longing feels like?" Chills went down my spine as I felt an intense, pent-up block of energy in my second chakra, like water behind a dam. This was a physical desire for sexual union like nothing felt in a human body. My heart burst forth with compassion as I realized just how similar horses were to humans.

It wasn't just about sex. Martie wanted a partner. She showed me images of colts and fillies, with a male horse standing by her side and the two of them nuzzling each other. I felt the desire in her heart that I knew was the same as my own. Like humans, horses have a strong need for connection to their species, either by having a family of their own or living on the same property as other horses. Unfortunately, they are not able to choose what kind of life they are going to live, but we can help by being willing to compromise. The least we can do is honor their yearning to be social beings, by giving them the time and space to be around other horses. Martie was already over twenty years old, and the owners of the ranch did not want to breed her, but she did have a number of gelding gentlemen callers.

These compromises and connections are essential. As I felt the grief over what Martie would never have, but truly wanted, I was reminded of another horse I met through a colleague at the ranch in California where Angel lived.

She was a young, opinionated, blue roan Quarter Horse, handsome and smart, and greatly representing an angry, misunderstood teenager. Everyone called her Blue. Blue was the lead mare of the herd at a boarding facility just down the street from Angel. The owner, Kris, wanted Blue to be happy. She loved participating in hunter-jumper shows, but Blue was often unpredictable during them. Occasionally, she would start bucking during the middle of an event. Because Kris was a competent rider, she was always able to stay on her, but the bucking affected their scores.

When I talked to Blue, I felt in my heart that she loved the competition as well as the connection she had with Kris in the events they participated in. Her sleek, muscular physique showed her physical capability, and she had tenacious willpower and a serious personality that seemed aligned with a competitive lifestyle. When I stood before her, I felt so much vigor and vitality in my body, it made me want to bust out and run. Blue was well suited on all levels for this type of career!

But there was something wrong. She searched my face with large eyes and muddled energy. I asked her to tell me what was going on. I heard the words "no one understands." I saw a picture of a family of horses, and someone loading her up in a trailer and taking her away. She retreated to the back of the trailer, head lowered in sadness, tension from fear in her shoulders and neck. When I told Kris what I saw and asked about where Blue came from, she told me she was removed from her original herd, and sold to a retired rancher in the area. Because Blue had so much energy, the rancher sold her to Kris, who would be able to give her more of the exercise she needed. This all made sense. She was an angry, grieving horse who was whisked away from her family with no notice.

I asked Kris where they kept Blue before the show started. It did not surprise me to hear that it was a barn full of horses. No wonder she bucked during the race; like a rebellious teenager, she was fighting to not be taken away from her kind! Blue also bucked every once in awhile when she was ridden at the neighbor's ranch by a close friend of Kris's, who helped in her care. But this usually happened at the beginning of their ride, just after leaving the warm, cozy, social scene of her barn, and all her favorite friends. After realizing what was going on for Blue, I explained to her why she was taken away from her original family. I offered some healing energy—light and color—into the area of her heart chakra, helping her release the grief related to losing her original herd.

I told her that I would work with Kris to find a way to allow her to spend more quality time with the horses around her. Kris agreed to give her additional time with her herd at the boarding facility, outside the barn. I worked on a deal with Blue that if she was given more time with her horse family, she would in return respect Kris during their riding time together at the shows, as well as her neighbor who helped her get exercise next door. It proved to be a work in progress, and when Kris decided to trailer Blue a few miles from the shows for awhile, to see if Blue would stop associating their time there as a social engagement, she did report a decrease in the bucking.

As I left the workshop, I ruminated on the experiences of Blue and Martie. Martie's parting words echoed in my mind: "Do you know where he is?" I remembered the information given to me by the workshop horses in New Jersey. Was my partner, my mate, really here in England? If so, how would I meet him? They had directed me to go here, yet I had not run into anyone. I had hoped I would discover some work opportunities while in the area, but there was nothing available at the ranch where the workshop was held or in any of the surrounding ranches or farms I had visited. My heart was heavy and downcast, like the gloomy clouds that persisted throughout my time there. I did not feel a calling to move to England. In fact, the energy felt discordant with my own, and I longed for home in California. I wondered what the horses had meant. Why England?

Perhaps it was all a growth experience. I had gained confidence in working with people, and learned to trust my intuition, become more aware of my gifts, and let my power shine through. As Adele, Marlena, and Thomas McCormick explained in *Horses and the Mystical Path*, things don't always go as expected as we walk our spiritual path. "The spiritual way is not about personal success, effectiveness, or glory. It is about being tenacious and optimistic, even when the odds seem to be clearly against us... and is ultimately character enhancing."[7]

The unexpected, magical surge of energy that helped me along in dire moments while in England was still a mystery to me. What I did know was that it was the cornerstone of my healing and transformation, and would eventually lead to all that my heart desired, in work, love, and spirituality. My next steps would be about building, accessing, and channeling it more effectively and with conscious intent, to benefit my life and the lives of others.

PART TWO

HORSES ARE HEALERS AND TEACHERS

CHAPTER FIVE

RECONCILIATION AND REBIRTH

After returning from England, I continued to gain more experience in several EFL sessions and workshops. I was also in the process of forming a partnership with another equine therapy facilitator, and there were many ups and downs as we worked out the details. I hung in there while things were uncertain and doubtful, because I really wanted to do this work.

I also had a series of dreams that revealed there was more than one potential mate for me at this time. One was a blurry version of a fisherman along the coast of what looked like the North Sea, not far from what I recognized as the area of Norfolk county; another was a tall, dark-haired coastal Californian, with a large, gray dragon tattoo on his right arm. I was unsure what to do about the first guy, since I'd been to England and back without seeing him; and as for the second one, I had not run into him yet. I decided that perhaps these were simply wish dreams—manifestations of my unconscious desire to meet my beloved.

All this time, I had continued with my nursing work at the hospital. The worst part of the period after I returned from England was that I was growing increasingly tired and intolerant of it. Ever since the original, initiating horse workshop, I had no more desire or motivation to continue in that line of work. It was not my soul's passion or purpose, and the long twelve-hour days wore down my body and mind. I had completed a degree in psychology, but decided the counseling world was not the right fit for me either. I was frustrated with all these false starts and incessant stops, and was ready to do what excited and invigorated me. The dissolution of the past left me with an eagerness to get going in my new vocation. The question was: when? That was a mystery. I knew there were no definite answers right now.

One day I walked into a coffee shop and as I ordered my drink I felt my heart skip a few beats. I looked up and before me was standing a very tall and handsome, dark-haired young man with a large, gray dragon tattoo on his right forearm. Along with the initial shock, I noticed my heart felt lighter and warmer. A feeling of excitement and desire raced through me as my energy linked with his. We exchanged just a few sentences of small talk, and then I quickly left, feeling unprepared and insecure after this unexpected meeting.

I went back to the coffee shop a few more times. I never saw that man again. I could not figure it out. He was clearly the man from my dream, so obviously the universe had thrown us together. What was going on?

A friend of mine told me about a Reiki Master named Renée who had helped her with some life difficulties. I was hoping for some clarity, so I went to see Renée. That's when I was introduced to the world of energy healing—healing through the human energy field or aura. It was in this first session that Renée told me to take a break and heal. She said that when the time was right, I would be filled with ideas and clarity about what actions to take to move forward in my work. For now, I should rest and be patient; my time would come soon enough.

She also said that both men in the dream were potential mates, but after visiting England, I unconsciously chose
California as the place where I wanted to reside. The man I met
at the coffee shop was the California man from the dream, but
at the moment of meeting him and the connection of our hearts,
my soul decided he was not the one best suited for me in my
journey ahead. He had done some healing and transformation
in the past, but was now content to stay put. Change would not
be something he was likely to engage in, which would make it
difficult for us to stay together. My own metamorphosis would
create too much distance between us.

With Renée's help, I looked at my lack of readiness for a conscious relationship, cleared those blocks, and called in my highest
potential mate. I was beginning to realize that potentials were just
possibilities that could always change as I healed, developed, and
made new decisions about what I wanted in my life. This time I
wanted no precognitive hits on what was to come—not from the
horses or anyone! It caused too much anticipation when making
decisions and taking action, leading to discouragement if things
didn't work out. I had decisions to make about steps to take in
my new vocation, where to live, and dating; and I wanted to make
those decisions from within, in accordance with my soul's evolution, not from my ego's desire for a mate.

In this session, I also healed and cleared even more of the
emotional pain and struggles that I had carried from my childhood—fear, insecurity, victimhood, self-doubt, and mistrust. I was
beginning to see clearly where I was headed in my life and vocation, not just in working with horses, but also with my abilities as
an intuitive and healer. I became aware that much of the emotional baggage I had carried throughout my life was partially blocking
the release of the healing energy from my chakras, preventing the
expression of my full potential.

In subsequent healing sessions with Renée as well as with other energy practitioners, I got more in touch with the degree of my empathic abilities. I always knew I was sensitive, and would easily react to the emotions of others. But I had no idea that I picked up and carried many of the vibrations of the influential people around me growing up, to the extent of taking on some of their feelings, physical sensations, thoughts, and life lessons. I thought I was just angry for what I went through personally.

Through working with the horses and Renée, and attending a transformational Tibetan Buddhist empowerment weekend, I was finally able to connect to my family again. I had reached a point where I had no resistance or unwillingness. I claimed complete responsibility for my feelings and perspectives, with the understanding that all I really needed was my own love and support. I didn't need anyone else to acknowledge or validate me in any way.

I will never forget the weekend that I reconnected with my family. After attending the Tibetan Buddhist empowerment the previous weekend, I reached out by email to the Lama who led the empowerment, sharing my struggle with making the decision to reunite with my family. I received a quick response from her. Her words were branded in my mind from that day on. She said, "You won't have to be angry anymore. You will be a blessing to your family and others in your life by radiating the truth with compassion and love. Because of your life experience, you will use the power of your love to help prevent others from creating negative karma through your seeing, knowing, and sensing."

I knew there was a reason I felt lighter, happier, and free, without having any logical understanding of how this occurred. I also knew it was no coincidence that my brother called me up just hours after I received the Lama's email. He was the father of a baby girl. I was returning to my biological family just in time to be an aunt!

In discovering that much of the anger I had carried in my past belonged to others, I was able to make sense of why it had taken so long to heal the wounds with Ken and my family. Through consistent self-awareness and discernment, in time I developed more mastery of knowing whether my feelings, sensations, thoughts, or other vibrations belonged to me. As I continued to release what wasn't mine, I watched those around me become increasingly aware of their own thoughts, feelings, and physical sensations. Although this causes discomfort for many, as Daniel Goldman summarized in his book *Emotional Intelligence: Why It Can Matter More Than IQ*, awareness is the first step in being able to take responsibility for, and begin healing one's life.

EMPATHIC REACTIVITY IN HORSES
Lessons for Making the Unconscious Conscious

Merriam-Webster's online dictionary defines empathy as "vicariously experiencing the feelings, thoughts, and experience of another of either the past or present without having the feelings, thoughts, and experience fully communicated in an objectively explicit manner."[1] This empathic ability is something also experienced by horses. Horses feel our emotions, sense our thoughts, absorb our energy, and act out all of these, including our behavior patterns. They can even take on our physical illnesses, to the point of death.

The horse workshops and training taught me exactly how a horse could behave in the presence of an incongruent human. Most horse owners are aware of how the main emotions—fear, anger, and sadness—manifest in a horse. Bolting, bucking, and withdrawing from our presence are their common reactions to our fervent feelings. You'd be less likely to see these behaviors, or extreme forms of them, if you are grounded, present, and actively processing your emotions. To do this, start by becoming aware of what you are truly feeling. Each time you interact with your horse, tap into the emotions, and any thoughts or sensations associated with them. If you make this a daily habit, even the heaviest of energies related to devastating traumas and wounding will eventually lighten and release from your energy field.

At the ranch where I rode Angel, it was commonplace to hear that someone's horse was crazy or skittish, or that they had a stubborn one on their hands. After getting to know many of these humans, it often occurred to me that these were qualities of the humans, not the horses. The horses were simply responding empathically to the unacknowledged thoughts, feelings, physical sensations, and behavior patterns of their human owners.

As Wyatt Webb described in his book based on his experiences with horses, *It's Not About the Horse*, an aggressive, pushy, or impatient human will find himself perpetually chasing his horse, especially when he is short on time. These are the people who can't get a halter on their horse when they need to because their energy pushes the horse away. Some people with these qualities, especially those unfamiliar with horses, think horses don't like them because they are always going off in the other direction, never wanting to stand next to them or be in their presence. The truth is, it's nothing personal; the horses are simply responding to energy.

From all my direct experience with horses, I can say that in opposition to an aggressive person, an overly passive person holds no sense of boundaries in his energy fields. These people find themselves in the presence of horses who walk all over them—literally.

And the horses are always right in their face—usually uncomfortably so. I remember another horse person at the ranch where I rode Angel, named Sera, telling me about her situation with her horse, Zybon. When she first got him, she had no horsemanship experience and was afraid of him. Sera would go to his paddock to feed him, and he would be up at the gate, pushing against her as she tried to walk in. Sometimes he even ran past her and out the gate, knocking her over in the process. Because of this pattern, Sera often threw his food over the gate, and got out of the area as quickly as possible. She felt like she had to be a "good mom," and not ask him to back up, listen to her, or allow her to care for him. Half the time, she could not even groom him without being pushed around the paddock!

Sera began taking riding lessons and horsemanship classes to learn how to interact with her horse, demand respect, and assert herself, which did help. But Sera told me what helped the most was the work she did for herself in psychotherapy. She began to look at similar patterns she had with people, especially men. Sera was beaten by her father throughout her childhood. He also over-powered her during her adulthood—demanding that she live the life he wanted her to have.

Unfortunately, for most of her life she unhappily complied. She chose occupations and relationships based on her father's dreams and expectations. Because of this early life experience and ingrained life pattern, Sera had been frequently bossed around by many other men in her work and love life. But because she now had begun to heal her past, Sera told me, she was experiencing a more graceful, easy, and balanced relationship with Zybon.

I told her about energy healing, and how it can help clear out the oldest, most unconscious issues from one's past, some of which are not even from this life. That is one of the most beneficial aspects of alternative or holistic healing. It works on a multidimensional level, addressing emotional, mental, physical, spiritual, and energetic aspects of ourselves at the same time. It also uncovers the root cause of an issue, healing its origin, so these emotions, thoughts, belief systems, or physical illnesses don't recur. Chinese medicine, homeopathy, bodywork, chiropractic, and Ayurveda are other examples of healing systems that focus on the causes of "dis-ease" rather than the symptoms.

Our culture has been imbued with the old, outdated tradi-tional medical system of putting a metaphoric band-aid over a wound and hoping it will disappear. There is definitely a time and place for traditional medicine, especially when it comes to injuries or, in some cases, infections or surgical procedures. But if we focus on the underlying cause of disease we can free ourselves from the prison of ongoing medications, and the need for lifelong therapy or invasive medical procedures that are required because the origi-nal wound was never dealt with or worsened with time.

Whether the horse is feeling your emotions, reading your mind, or mirroring your relationship dynamics, the most impor-tant thing to do, as Sera learned, is to take responsibility for your own healing. Do what you need to do to heal your mind and emotions, or your physical body if you are ill or stressed.

It is also essential to be in the present moment when you are around your horse. In my healing work, I always instruct clients to begin by taking two deep belly breaths, and grounding to the earth. You can then go through a self-awareness check-in, based on Linda Kohanov's body scan from *Riding Between the Worlds*.[2] This is done by tuning into your body from head to toe, becom-ing aware of any physical sensations, thoughts, emotions, images, sounds, colors, or even memories that come up when you focus on each area. After you receive this knowledge from your body, you will want to ask your Divine Self for more information.

The Divine Self is the pure, eternal aspect of your being that exists within your body's core. As described in *The Chela and the Path: Keys to Soul Mastery in the Aquarian Age*, dictated by Elizabeth Clare Prophet, the Divine Self is a wise, all-know-ing aspect of our being, one who assists and guides us on our life path. You can make contact with this part of your being, by bringing your attention to the light in the center of your heart chakra.

Through your intent, you will access your Divine Self. You might see, feel, or sense it in a particular way, which is perfectly appropriate. This will be unique for each person. If you don't notice anything, use your imagination to make contact. Contact can be made more easily if you keep an open mind and take a leap of faith, especially if this is new to you. If your personal beliefs, religion, or upbringing make it difficult for you to comprehend a Divine Self, you can think of it as a higher power. Visualize this higher power making contact with your physical body. Then bring your attention to this place.

When you connect with this divinity, you should receive information in a way that makes sense to you—a way that expands upon your body's original messages.

The check-in will help you become grounded, centered, and focused in your body. Messages from spirit can come through the body more clearly and easily when you are completely present, even for those who are not intuitively inclined. As Deepak Chopra wrote in his article "Just Listen! Your Body is Speaking To You," "The issues are in the tissues."[3] When you bring your attention to your physical body, you can acknowledge and take responsibility for whatever is going on within. As you do, the issues begin to shift, which lessens the amount and intensity that a horse will pick up on.

This even helps decrease the chances that your horse will read your mind when you don't want him to, like when changing gaits. Be in the present moment and think about cantering only when you are ready to canter. This is prime training for all areas of your life. Many times we become confused when we try to plan things in the future, unsure of what is to come. We start obsessing over things that have not happened yet. It is best if we stay attuned to the now. This will prevent us from going out of balance or alignment, from jumping ahead and throwing off our own timing.

Much of the confusion that goes on with riding has to do with the ceaseless, chaotic thoughts of humans. We are not always clear about what we want to do, and are often flooded with conflicting, multi-layered, and irrelevant thoughts. How can we expect our horses to know what to do when we have these mixed messages floating around in our minds, which many times have nothing to do with the task at hand?

Understanding this idea can help us begin to see the value in becoming more aware of our thoughts and controlling what we think about in every moment. Personal experience has taught me that meditation is a great tool for helping humans become more aware of the diversity of thoughts that rumble through our minds, as well as how to calm and quiet the mind, leading to more presence and focus in everyday activities.

MIRANDA AND RORY
Releasing Trauma and Gaining Insight

A couple years after the workshop in England, a friend called me, wanting my intuitive advice about her horse. Miranda currently worked part-time at one of the local metaphysical bookstores. She was wondering about her horse, Rory, and his chronic bouts of diarrhea that did not respond to antacids or probiotics. She was also going through a huge financial transition. She had sprained her ankle, and was on medical leave from her book delivery job, so the work at the bookstore was her only source of income. Because of this, Miranda didn't know if she could even afford to keep Rory.

When she did the self-awareness check-in, she was able to identify tightness in her throat and pain in her lower belly. After consulting her Divine Self for further information about these sensations, Miranda discovered that she was really sad and scared. She explained that a good friend had moved away a few months ago. She had known about it for months beforehand, and after it happened she thought she was fine. With just a few tears shed, they had agreed to keep in touch. But now, just in the check-in, she was already crying and feeling the sadness from missing her friend.

Miranda asked her Divine Self about her belly pain, and got just that—the word pain. I received an immediate, intuitive hit right away. I asked her if she ever had trouble with her digestion. It turned out that she had been diagnosed with Crohn's disease years ago, but had been without symptoms for the last six months. I immediately considered the empathic link between her and Rory. I also sensed that much of Miranda's Crohn's disease was caused by built-up emotional trauma from her past, and that the sadness she was feeling was more than just about a friend who moved away. I didn't reveal any of this to her yet. I wanted to watch how she interacted with Rory, and tune in to him to discover what could be causing the diarrhea.

Miranda walked into a nearby pasture where Rory was grazing. My intention was to help Miranda discover her own truths and offer some feedback; it wasn't my plan to do a structured EFL session. But now I watched with curiosity as Rory and some other horses in the pasture stepped up to the plate to help Miranda. As soon as Rory approached her, Miranda burst into tears. The other horses surrounded her. She sat underneath a nearby tree and continued to weep as the horses stood near her. Each horse came up one by one, licking, chewing, and lowering their heads with eyes of watery wells reflecting her sorrow.

This is one magical way that I have found horses heal us energetically. All animals have permeable energy fields, easily absorbing all that radiates and resounds around them. This is true of the entire natural kingdom. This is why we feel more relaxed and rejuvenated after a swim in the ocean or a walk through a meadow. Our negativity melts into Mother Nature, which lightens our load and can be transmuted into a form that benefits her. It is a natural symbiotic balance. Our physical bodies are purified in the process.

Horses make licking and chewing movements with their mouths when they are comfortable in your presence. As Monte Roberts explained in his book *The Man Who Listens To Horses*, this action in horses is also a sign of their submission to you. I have observed that horses will also lick and chew when a human in their presence is aware of and actively experiencing his emotional, mental, and physical body processes. The licking and chewing motion they make represents the physical way they help us release the energies we are processing, on all levels of our being. This is why we often feel better after spending time with horses, especially when we have been suffering from mental anguish or emotional distress. The horses work in the same way that Mother Nature does, absorbing these heavy or negative energies. It is for this reason that I refer to them as energy workers. They certainly help us shift our energy.

I have postulated a couple reasons why some animals get sick from absorbing our energies and the energies of other beings in the world, and others do not. The first idea has to do with our consciousness. The more conscious we are of whatever is going on inside of us, no matter how intense it is, the less they are impacted by it, and the easier it is for them to transmute it or release it from their energy fields. The animal and nature kingdoms will be less negatively affected by our mental/emotional states if we can on some level acknowledge and work through them. The more we can feel our pain, the less likely our animals will become ill.

If we are unaware of our emotions and the thoughts associated with them, or we become overwhelmed by their intensity, these uncontained energies leak out of our energy fields into our natural absorbing animal and nature companions. If these emotional bouts are not frequent, the animal or area of nature can still transmute the heavy energy and they won't become sick. But after repeated exposure, the toxic build-up of unconscious energy leaking out of humans can remain stagnant or sticky, like sludge, and the animal or nature area can no longer keep up with the transmutation or clearing process.

This is partly why our animals can develop illness due to our unhealthy mental/emotional states, and also why areas of the Earth have become so out of balance over time. However, because Mother Nature is vast and extensive, it takes the unconscious energy of large groups and collectives of humans to cause certain areas to become imbalanced. It is a process involving many over a period of time, in a particular area, that causes problems. We are meant to take refuge in our natural world. The responsibility for an unhealthy area of nature cannot rest with any one person, or even a few, no matter how emotional or unconscious.

Keep in mind that areas of Mother Nature can get out of balance or become diseased through other causes, such as pollution, chemical toxins, climate change, and overharvesting resources. Many natural disasters and weather changes are even a result of Earth's evolutionary process. When it comes to the influence of our energies, many aspects of nature are also protected in some ways, because they are not necessarily in close proximity to us, or emotionally attached to us like our own animals are. In addition, the spirit of Earth, Gaia, has great compassion for all who live on her.

This brings me to my second idea about why some animals become ill from absorbing our energies and others do not. It has to do with the bond between the human and animal. Animals are more like us than they are like nature, especially since they have become domesticated. Their immense love for us, which is often a major reason for their incarnation and coming into our lives, compels them to want to help us. In the process of picking up our energies, they might continue to hold on to them, which can lead to emotional and physical illnesses. Although they are naturally more compassionate than most humans because of their nonjudgmental natures, animals are still learning how to master compassion through the experience of their empathy. In this way, they can release the energies they absorb from us. The more compassionate they are, the less likely they are to become sick.

In the course of the development of their consciousness and evolution, animals will gain more mastery of compassion. However, animals learn about compassion in a different way than humans do—in a process that utilizes more of their energetic and emotional natures. The Merriam-Webster dictionary defines compassion as "sympathetic consciousness of others' distress together with a desire to alleviate it."[4] I will add that along with being deeply aware of another's experience, feeling and caring for them, compassion also involves understanding that the other being is living that experience for a specific purpose. It is the knowledge that taking on another's problem could interfere with their individual healing process, preventing them from learning life lessons and growing spiritually.

With compassion, one innately knows that he or she can help, but ultimately must allow that other being to move through their experience in their own way, even if they suffer in the process. In this way, those who are compassionate develop a sense of detachment by accepting and not rescuing the other. In *The Dalai Lama's Book of Love and Compassion*, he talked about how having compassion can benefit the one who is compassionate, as well as others, even our enemies. The energy of compassion purifies and cleanses on many levels, bringing health and wholeness to all parties.

Those animals who are more conscious of themselves as separate entities, including the awareness of their different levels of being—emotion, thought, and spirit—are also able to more easily clear empathic energy—the energy of others around them—so they don't become ill. This doesn't mean they understand the different levels of their being the same way we do. Their brains are different from ours in a variety of ways. With most animals, because of this lack of consciousness, the unfolding of their evolution, and their continual bombardment with the heavier energies in the world around them, we must do the clearing for them. I describe specific energy techniques for clearing an animal's energy fields in Chapter Twelve.

I reflected on these ideas as I observed Miranda in the field with Rory. I knew it was possible that his digestive disturbances were a result of absorbing her Crohn's disease. The loving bond between them was glaringly obvious in the way he laid down next to her, as she gently stroked his mane. Most of her tears had been shed, and she now sat in quiet contemplation. By the distant look in her eyes, I could see that she was still processing the thoughts and emotions moving through her. I asked Miranda to come back into the now and focus on the two sensations she tapped into during the check-in. As she did, Rory looked up at her, and the presence of energy returned to her sitting posture and into her eyes.

Miranda told me the tightness in her throat had eased up, but the pain in her belly persisted. I reminded her to breathe and continue to be with whatever came up emotionally, mentally, or physically. She nodded as a painful expression crossed her face—eyes tensed and eyebrows clenched together. The other horses had gone back out to pasture, but Rory was still lying next to her, yet giving both of them plenty of room to move about.

Horses aren't always comfortable lying down. As Chris Irwin discussed in his book *Horses Don't Lie: What Horses Teach Us About Our Natural Capacity For Awareness, Confidence, Courage, and Trust*, their prey nature causes them to need to be able to run off quickly if danger arises. Sitting or lying down is not an easy position to run from. Even though Rory was Miranda's horse, he still had to feel safe enough to willingly place himself in this vulnerable position, and I sensed this was happening because she was actively experiencing her healing process. She was not suppressing anything; therefore he could trust that what she was showing him externally—in her body posture, non-verbals, and actions—was based on what was truly happening internally. Even more, he could predict how she would respond based on the genuine processes she was moving through.

Even the horses in the pasture knew there would be no sudden attacks or hidden agendas, unlike with a human unconscious of his anger and fear. A horse in the presence of an unconscious human would feel these emotions, which would cause him to remain on guard, in a perpetual state of alarm, as if at any moment the human could fly into a rage and lash out.

This unconsciousness is often what causes humans to act out their emotions in ways that harm others. After having repressed and suppressed their emotions so deeply, all clear perspective and control is lost. The emotions have accumulated inside, usually after years of pushing them down. When this happens, many people experience unpredictable bouts of flooding, or an overwhelming inability to integrate the feelings. The stuffed emotions often surface due to a trigger, or something that is reminiscent of the original experience(s) that caused the emotions in the first place. The human will then act out according to his disposition—fight or flight. One person may run away or become withdrawn; another might lash out in words or physical violence.

I checked in with Miranda again. Her body appeared relaxed and her voice was strong, but not tense, therefore I knew she was in the present moment. She also checked in with the two areas, saying they felt lighter and she felt less emotional when she brought her awareness to them. I asked her if she felt ready to end the session. Distractedly, she mumbled that she needed to have a heart-to-heart with Rory.

Although I could not hear her, I recognized that Miranda was expressing something very important to Rory, by the stiffening of her body posture, flamboyant arm gestures moving from her heart to him, and fierce eye contact. A few chest-heaves later, more tears, and then Rory placed his head on her shoulder. She wrapped her arms around his neck and they held each other there for a while longer.

After Miranda came out of the pasture, I checked in about how this unplanned EFL session turned out for her. As I expected, Miranda shared that she thought much of her grief had more to do with other life events than it had to do with her friend moving away. When Rory first walked up to her, she remembered the pain of her parents' divorce as a child, especially the day she found out about it. Her mother had sat her down in her bedroom, telling her that her father would be leaving the house over the next few days, soon to live at his own place. She went on to explain more about why, but Miranda recalled the feeling of being frozen in place, as if paralyzed. She never got past the statement that her father was leaving the house.

She also reported the loss of a close friend in high school. Suzy and Miranda were the best of friends, meeting each day for lunch and in between classes, as well as spending time after school at each other's houses, watching TV and playing tennis. One day, she got a note from Suzy saying she didn't want to be friends anymore. That was it, no explanation, yet the end of all contact. Miranda again experienced the cold, numbing feeling of being frozen, like she did when her mother told her about the divorce.

In both instances, she didn't recall any other emotion, only shock. As we talked about her memories coming up while she was with the horses, Miranda realized that she had never fully processed these past traumas. She started to process the move of her most recent friend, but even that was stunted because of its resonance with older losses. They remained stuck inside of her, because earlier in her life she went into shock and had no tools to cope with reality. All of this grief she had experienced throughout her life had accumulated within, just waiting to be dealt with. And today it was finally released.

I asked Miranda if she thought any of this past trauma and grief built up over time could be related to her Crohn's disease. She told me she was starting to open up to the idea that many illnesses were related to unresolved emotional issues. I informed Miranda that as I have observed in many of my experiences with horses, they have a way of helping us unlock the trauma held in our nervous systems, releasing anything that has been halted in its unfolding. As Peter Levine wrote in his book *Waking the Tiger: Healing Trauma*, "The frozen residue of energy that has not been resolved and discharged...remains trapped in the nervous system where it can wreak havoc on our bodies and spirits.... We can thaw by initiating and encouraging our innate drive to return to a state of dynamic equilibrium."[5]

Because horses naturally hold a safe space, the emotions can be experienced, processed, and finally let go of, which is what I witnessed in Miranda's session. I wanted to keep in touch with her to see if she remained free of the symptoms of Crohn's. I felt that we got to the heart of the origin of the illness, unless there were other lingering issues.

As we ended the session that day, there was one mystery question left unanswered. I still wondered if Rory's symptoms were somehow related to Miranda's Crohn's disease, if in fact he had picked up some of her illness. Because Miranda received such a deep healing, I'd be curious to see if Rory's digestion improved in the future. In the meantime, I showed her techniques she could use to clear empathic energy from Rory's aura.

I had already learned much about being empathic; I educated Miranda about how animals instinctively pick up on our emotions, thoughts, physical sensations, and illnesses because of their bond with us. I further divulged that when people become aware of their issues, take responsibility for them and work them out on all levels, it lessens the load that their animals pick up and carry. Miranda seemed relieved by this, nodding her head in agreement. She felt that Rory had always tried to protect and comfort her, even now with the big transition she was making with her job.

Miranda shared with me the last conversation she had with Rory. She confessed her dilemma about keeping him. To her astonishment, she felt like he "told her in her head" that he had already known about her anguish in making this decision, and that he would be alright with whatever she did. It didn't surprise me, since I had already discovered from working with kids that horses pick up on our thoughts. She talked it out with him, and decided he could stay on her friend's pasture awhile, until she could get back on her feet financially.

The downfall was that her friend's pasture was two states away, so she wouldn't be able to visit him very often. But her friend lived on a farm, and there would be plenty of work for Rory to do, and other horses for him to hang out with. Miranda felt complete with the way the conversation ended, because his energy still felt positive, even when he put his head on her shoulder. That was when she knew he was comforting her and telling her it would be okay. I told her from my stance it looked like everything transpired smoothly, and that, based on his response to her, they had made the right decision together.

As I hugged Miranda goodbye and thanked her for the pleasure of working with her, I realized how amazed I was by the love and understanding of these glorious beings. A noble, loyal horse, Rory appeared to truly support his human in doing what was best in her situation, with total acceptance and non-attachment. I thought about how much Miranda processed her own life experiences in this session, including her emotional and physical issues. That is when it truly sank in—how powerfully healing and life-changing these sessions were! I realized that this was why my offering intuitive advice and instruction to a friend had shifted into an equine facilitated session. I needed to see how this process could naturally and unexpectedly unfold. I had so much fun. I couldn't wait for my next equine healing experience.

CHAPTER SIX

SELF-MASTERY AND BUILDING MY TRADE

Over the next few months I continued to work with Renée, healing more layers of the original traumas I experienced throughout my life. I was moving into a greater level of trust and empowerment. I was developing more confidence and compassion. Many of these wounds went back many lifetimes, where I was betrayed and victimized, sometimes by other healers and gurus.

An unexpected memory came through from another lifetime: I was sexually assaulted by a neighbor as a young child. I was shocked and horrified by this discovery. Fortunately, it was a faint memory, and the heavy energies I still carried from it weren't as intense as with some of the traumas I'd suffered in this life.

With energy work, I found I processed the emotions quickly and easily, and the trauma lifted out without any uncomfortable physical sensations or flashbacks. The hardest part was my mind—getting past the reality of what happened and making decisions about my relationships because of it. I learned that the soul of the abuser from that lifetime was incarnated in my life this time around, too, as my friend's brother. This explained why

I was confused by conflicting feelings about him, which included a sense of familiarity mixed with curiosity, and being repulsed by him for no apparent reason.

I realized that in clearing this trauma and the karma associated with it, I could begin to feel neutral toward him for the first time. I knew then that the relationship with my friend's brother would naturally come to an end or continue on in a healthy manner, and it didn't have to get resolved overnight. I could also relax more and enjoy the relationship with my friend, without it being tainted by the mixed feelings I had for her brother. More importantly, I was happy to be able to let go of another trauma that was holding me back from reaching my goals in my career and love life.

I also knew it was time to really get started in my chosen field of work. The time spent working at the hospital was growing more and more unbearable. I had dreams where I refused to do any of my daily tasks and yelled out in frustration. My body ached from physical exhaustion and my mind throbbed with boredom. I wanted to freely express my own creative ideas and healing. I was becoming impatient and overzealous, eager to build my new career with horses so I could quit my job and do this on a regular basis.

Disappointingly, the EFL partnership fell through due to conflicting work schedules and lack of a clientele. But I was grateful to have experienced a spontaneous practice session with my friend Miranda. Because there was no money exchanged there was no pressure on my end, yet at the same time I got to witness another example of the healing potential in this work. I became inspired to come up with a plan to do more of this work with another colleague. I needed to begin to set things in motion. I just didn't know how yet.

In the meantime, I came to the conclusion that my first step involved changing things up at the ranch. I learned all I could while riding Angel. It was time to experience riding a completely different horse. My intuition told me this would benefit me in more ways than one. And it was definitely not just about riding, as it never was.

MEETING TOMMY AND MY FEAR

One afternoon I asked Angel's owner if there was another horse available for me to ride for a while. I especially wanted to learn to lope, and Angel was getting older and had a shoulder injury that prevented it. Angel's owner introduced me to Katherine, the owner of Tommy, a nine-year-old bay Quarter Horse, who was a manly gelding, through and through. Katherine used Tommy primarily for lessons with kids, and said he was a strong, reliable horse for adults as well, especially for improving and learning more advanced riding skills.

I spent some time in front of Tommy's stall, tuning in to him to see if there was a connection between us—making sure that we both wanted to participate in this partnership. He responded to me right away, making full eye contact, lowering his head easily, and snorting and nickering. I asked him if he wanted to spend some time together, getting to know each other better. I felt a resounding *yes* inside, as I watched him rub up against the fence of his stall, awaiting my next move.

As soon as we began activities together, I knew this was going to be an experience like no other. Like every horse—and every human—Tommy was unique in his personality, strengths, and weaknesses. I knew I needed to approach and work with him accordingly, adjusting the way I interacted with him to provide the best possible outcome for both of us.

Tommy took charge in a very dominant, willful, all-business way. From the beginning, he was on a mission—his own mission. I led him out of his stall and he pulled me from stall to stall, visiting with his friends and eating grass and alfalfa bordering the other horses' stalls. Obviously, this was a horse who would teach me how to move more fully into my power.

I finally got him tied to the hitching posts that surrounded the arena. I checked my fear level, which had risen in this new experience, calming myself down in the process. Tommy was subdued for the moment. I began to talk to him and groom him. He relaxed into the process and began to look at me with curiosity. It seemed like a peculiar experience for him, which surprised me since he worked with kids regularly. He was probably more familiar with experienced riders in both kids and adults, those who had conquered their fears, or in the case of some kids, those who might not have had the chance for fear and self-doubt to slip into their worldview yet. If they grew up riding horses and had reasonable, healthy authority figures around them, they most likely believed there wasn't anything they couldn't do.

I thought I had my hands full with Tommy. To my surprise, when I finally got him in the riding arena he wasn't pushy any more. In the first lesson I had with him, he was actually pretty slow and predictable, much like Katherine had described. Katherine worked with me in this lesson, to make sure both Tommy and I felt safe and comfortable with one another. We went around the riding arena at a walk and then an easy jog. I found it a bit arduous to get him to follow commands. I had to use extra emphasis with my voice and energy when asking him to change gaits and direction. Yet it still went smoothly for the most part.

The real test was the lope, a slow and quiet three-beat gait in Western style riding. After mastering the first two gaits in English style with Angel—walk and trot, including learning how to post, which is to bob up and down in the saddle in rhythm with a horse's trotting gait, I was ready for the next riding skill. My goal for riding was not dressage, which is a type of competition often referred to as horse ballet. Dressage involves the rider's guiding a horse through a series of complex, precise, and delicate leg maneuvers. I was not interested in hunter-jumper, where horse and rider are tested on their ability, speed, and style of maneuvering through a set-up course of a variety of jump heights.

My main goal was to connect with horses, enjoying the mutual and sensual pleasure of moving together as one. I found that with the close contact that riding involves, both horse and human have the potential to develop a compassion and understanding for each other that is extremely healing and freeing on so many levels. Depending on how deep the horse and human decide to connect to one another in each riding experience, each species is given the chance to glimpse or embrace the other's soul through a willingness to be receptive, cooperative, and adaptive with each movement of riding.

I gripped and rubbed the horn of the saddle with nervousness as I sat on Tommy, wondering what would happen next as I prepared for the lope. Katherine went over with me what to expect. "Go in a straight line for now, it's easier to maintain your balance in the saddle," she said. "Breathe, let go, and feel the horse underneath you, and you'll do fine."

I took a deep breath and tensed up inside with expectation. I called out to Tommy, asking for a lope. Nothing happened. I sat more upright in the saddle, trying to make sense of the lack of action. Katherine encouraged me to try it again, and to kick with my right leg, which was the loping cue he was taught in his training. "LOPE!" I called out, kicking at the same time. Again, nothing. Tommy stood as still as a statue. I tried it a few more times, still with no forward movement, not even a step. I wondered if it would be easier to glide into the lope from a jog, rather than ask for it from a standstill position. After repeatedly trying to get to the lope from a jog without any success, I was ready to give up. Katherine offered the suggestion that it was possible

Tommy was not willing to lope because he was picking up on my fear, the part of me that did not want to lope.

I slumped over in temporary defeat as I recalled all the reasons why I might fear the unknown gait. This new uncharted experience with Tommy was risky because we would be moving faster than before. It was also a different rhythm than a walk or jog, and I had no idea if I would be able to stay balanced in the saddle. There was no way to minimize the newness of the experience in a practice or warm-up routine. I just had to do it. And yes, I could fall and get hurt.

Sadness and disappointment washed over me. All the other things I feared in my life bubbled up in my mind, thoughts of a new relationship and career change. Was I still afraid of rejection, getting hurt, or failing with either one of them—or both? What if I was blocking success in either of these areas because I was still too afraid of the risks or even going beyond my comfort zone?

I thought of how tormented I was by the idea of having to continue working at the hospital for years into the future. I also thought of how much my heart longed for a partner in life. I wanted someone for companionship, to be sensual and intimate with, both physically and emotionally. It had already been five years since I was with Ken, my last relationship. I recalled one of my most recent healing sessions where I called in my next highest potential mate, becoming excited and primed for that depth of connection with another. There was no way I was going to let fear get in the way now!

I was determined to experience the lope with Tommy. I sat upright again, took a deep breath in, and exhaled it through my solar plexus and root chakra, connecting to Tommy's solar plexus located just underneath the saddle. Assuredly and with might, I asked him for the lope again.

This time he took off. In amazement and relief, I felt Tommy move beneath me in a graceful, rocking chair motion. I was completely present, noticing my body shift in the saddle and slide back into balance again. With my body and focused vision, I directed him straight ahead. I was smiling and having fun as together we seemed to bounce and dance upon the earth. And before I knew it, it was over. It didn't take long for Tommy to reach the other side of the arena.

When I dismounted, I was beaming. It was a day of success. I had overcome my fear, and for me it was more than just a fear of loping for the first time. I was certain other fears had been worked out as well, in just the few minutes we spent together at the lope. I thanked Katherine for her help. She concluded it was safe for me to ride Tommy on my own from here on out, as long as other people were around the ranch. I was looking forward to having my own chance to work with Tommy alone, discovering what else he had to teach me.

Over the course of the next month, I started investigating horse ranches and organizations that provided EFL work, taking my next step in getting things going. I talked to many horse trainers, riding instructors, and equine therapy facilitators who gave me information and resources. No one was looking for any of the help I could offer right now, but they would let me know if something changed. It was suggested that I attend specific fundraisers and workshops, networking with others interested in this same field, thereby promoting myself. I did attend a few, but again had no luck for a real, concrete start.

Then one day I had a breakthrough. I found a farm in a nearby city that was looking for help to feed, clean stalls, and administer medications to their twenty horses. I also found a horse rescue in Orange County, California, that was looking for someone to help care for their horses. On a whim, I asked the owner of the rescue if I could do healing work with the horses there, as many of them were abandoned, abused, or neglected.

I was confident because I had learned some techniques from a shaman I worked with during my time in psychotherapy. He taught me how to heal with my hands, pulling off the energies hindering another's health or well-being. I had also gained experience from working with Renée. Many of the energy healing protocols and universal laws that were used in my sessions could be applied just the same to heal animals. I shared this with the owner of the rescue, and I also told her what I had learned through the workshops and trainings in EFL—how horses could help people heal. She was more than happy to have me on board. This was a volunteer situation only, but I was overjoyed to be moving forward.

JASPER
An Unfriendly Horse

I started working at the farm first. It was located on ten acres of beautiful rolling hills. This facility provided an opportunity for me to gain practical skills in caring for twenty horses with many different backgrounds. I learned all about the different nutrient requirements and types of food for horses. I also gained experience giving them their medicines and supplements, becoming educated about those commonly used. After feeding, medicating, and cleaning their stalls, I put their blankets on them in cold weather, tucking them in for the night.

One horse in particular stands out in my memory. Jasper became a retired racehorse at a very early age. His owner had put him through a rigorous schedule and training, and one day he snapped, throwing his rider during a competition. That was the end of his working days.

Jasper was a skinny, buckskin Thoroughbred with a mean look in his eye that sent shivers down my spine. I feared him at first sight. I also didn't like him. This was new for me when it came to horses. The feeling seemed to be mutual, but not personal towards me. When I met him, I stood there taking all of him in, discerning what was going on in that tortured mind of his. I knew he had the ability to immediately size someone up, deciding how he would control the situation, even before he made a move.

In that brief moment of meeting, I could sense the wheels inside his mind churning, planning. Along with the mean look was a slight shoulder tilt and shift of his weight that was followed by a flickering of his ears. I quickly learned that when I saw these signs it was one of his bad days, and I needed to be extra careful in my interactions with him. He could never be trusted, but on those days I couldn't take any chances.

The icy rocks in my gut always told me so. Even when he didn't display the tilting and flickering it was clear he did not trust humans; he would lash out at them any chance he could get, before they hurt him. I experienced this firsthand when I entered his paddock. It was testing time. When I carried his food into the paddock, he began to eat from the bucket before I got it in his feeder. He also tried to push me around in this process, and ended up biting me in the back of the leg. The bite hardly broke the skin and didn't draw blood, but I was still shocked and scared. I was definitely not comfortable with this kind of behavior and didn't want it to continue. I did not feel safe with his intentional disrespect of my boundaries. On top of this, I had the feeling that he would kick me if I was anywhere near his backside. I realized I needed to do something right away. In the midst of that first feeding, I haltered him and tied him to the gate while I finished getting the remainder of his food in the feeder.

After such a troublesome start with Jasper, I knew I needed to make a change in how I interacted with him, or risk having his behavior continue and possibly escalate for the worse. Because I started off with fear from the moment I met him, he knew he already had the upper hand. He was aware of this weakness in me, and he was the dominant bully in the herd that consisted of him and me. I knew I needed to deal with my fear.

Using the energy techniques I had learned, I transmuted my fear into faith and trust. From that time on, I went into his stall holding a different stance. I had to continue to work on it regularly, at times re-experiencing the fear. Usually I would strengthen the tone in my voice or carry a lunge whip as a physical barrier for assistance, asking him firmly to back out of my space before he could get too close or bite.

I made steady progress with Jasper, but sometimes he would still come up behind me while I was cleaning the stall or obtaining the horses' medications, bite at my shirt, or sneak his head around my shoulder. With another horse, it might feel okay, even affectionate, but with Jasper I still didn't feel safe. Sometimes I would tell him to back off, with anger blasting through my words. He would react to this, usually running off, but not before trying to lash out. He would push me with his head or snap his jaws for a bite.

One day I finally realized that I was taking his behavior personally and that he knew I didn't like him. That's when a light bulb went on in my head. Jasper was just an insecure, untrusting horse who mostly lived in a state of reactivity because he was hurt and traumatized by his past. I began to feel for him, realizing that he had never received the healing he needed, and was perpetually in a state of defending himself against all humans. The only solace he had was with the other horses, although most of the horses stayed away from him. But he didn't have the mean look or lash out at them the way he did with me or any other human.

I knew how to work with energy to help others release past trauma, as well as receive the complete lesson from the trauma, and shift residual emotions. After receiving permission from the farm owner, I decided to do some healing with Jasper, giving him the tools and resources to shift out of the trap he found himself in with every human. I did the healing work from inside his stall, but not laying a hand on him. I could do this easily through intent and the directing of the healing energies to his energy fields. Jasper would calm and the tension in his shoulders, ears, and overall body would diminish or even disappear. I always did the energy work with Jasper after I finished my chores for the day. It was a nice way to end my time with him, and it also felt right leaving on a good note.

Over the next few months while I worked with him, my compassion grew, because now I knew he had tools that could help him change his thoughts, feelings, and behavior. I realized that Jasper, like everyone else, went through his earlier life experiences for a reason. He could move beyond his previous limitations if his soul chose to.

My personal feelings about him also started to shift. A soft spot bloomed inside for what he had gone through, and I began to admire his soul's courage to triumph over his life's circumstances. Because his behavior began to change, I felt safer around him. The safety allowed me to put my guard down, and feel more loving and affectionate towards him. In return, Jasper picked up on the fact that I no longer disliked him, and so he felt safer with me. It became a win-win situation. As the fear between us continued to lessen, and the compassion strengthened, he became more comfortable and less aggressive in my presence. The mean look, tilt of the shoulder, and flickering ears were seen less. But there were also times where he had relapses, especially with other people who worked with him and had anger and fear in his presence.

TRUST
A Necessary Quality for Success

I continued to ride Tommy while I worked at the horse farm over the course of one winter. Things were going very well with riding. I was beginning to feel more confident with each ride. After riding in the arena for a while, I wanted to begin to ride on the trails with Tommy. I expected that trail riding would become one of my favorite horse activities because being with horses in a natural setting always felt playful and relaxing to me. My experiences thus far with being out on the trails with Angel had been pleasurable and invigorating, yet healing for both of us. On top of this, arena riding was starting to feel monotonous to me, and I was ready for something new.

My first trail ride with Tommy was unforgettable. I went with one of the local boarders who was an experienced rider, since this was my first time on the trails with Tommy. We started off at the walk, as usual, getting into the groove of the trails. After being out for some time on the path, we decided to lope. I had always wanted to try this on the trails. Cecelia, the woman I was riding with, took the lead on her horse Maverick, and began the lope.

As is typical for horses, Tommy followed the lead of the horse in front, by immediately moving into the lope. I was surprised at how quickly and easily he switched gears, much like a car with automatic transmission does when you press down on the gas pedal. I didn't have to be overly willful in my intent or energy to get him to go this time. We were off with lightning speed down the trail. A stream of joy whisked through my being, as I felt free in our flight.

But then Maverick picked up speed and it felt like he was about to break into a run. I was comfortable in the relaxed rocking mode of loping, but the increased tempo caught me off guard. As Tommy cruised ahead, I felt myself start to lose balance in the saddle.

Fear shot through me like the sudden firing of a gun. I instinctively grabbed the saddle horn to hold on and switched the reins to one hand. I was falling forward and sideways now, trying to duck my head to avoid hitting the tree branches we were flying under. I became immobilized with the fear that Tommy wouldn't stop because he was following Maverick's pace.

Finally, I forced open my own mouth and called out to Cecelia to slow down. Like the great riding buddy she already was, she slowed Maverick in that instant. Both horses switched into a fast trot and then down to the walk again. I took a deep breath of relief. We were safe. But that was a heck of a ride!

The rest of the ride was uneventful, until we reached the ridge that took us on a gravel road overlooking the city. It was a pleasant wide road, surrounded by avocado and orange trees, without any hikers around. The best part was that it was uphill. Cecilia asked if I wanted to lope again. I hesitated at first, being content with the fact that I had just survived our rapid jaunt.

But then I figured: why not! Practice makes perfect. In a moment's notice Cecilia and Maverick were off again. This time Tommy started to lunge forward as if into the lope, but instead remained in a quick trot. I nudged his side with my right heel, urging him forward with my body and words. "Go, Tommy. Go!" I felt his body rev up underneath me like a car's engine, and knew he wanted to follow my request, but he remained in the trot. Cecilia slowed down ahead and asked how it went. I told her we were both fine but we didn't go into the lope. "Want to try again?" she asked.

The momentum from the forward movement of the horses zipped through me again as they began to take off. I was beginning to understand the true meaning of "horse power." Tommy quickly went into the trot, but held back on the lope. I repeatedly urged him to lope as before, through my words, body, and energy. That was when I heard his voice in my head. He said, "Do you trust me?" Without thinking, the words suddenly slipped from my mouth, "Yes...yes, I want to do this, but don't go too fast." Then his words in my mind again, "You have to let go."

I automatically inhaled and from deep inside my core, I let go of my fear. I had to begin to trust that Tommy would help keep me balanced in the saddle, as well as follow my cue to slow down or stop. As I felt this trust emerge, Tommy gracefully moved into the lope. I breathed and felt him underneath me, knowing I was completely supported and safe. I remembered that we were going uphill this time too, so it was much easier to maintain balance than on flat ground or downhill. With this realization, I eased up and felt excitement run through me as we continued loping ahead. Cecelia turned around on Maverick, looking back at me and asking how I was. "Great," I smiled. "This is the best lope yet." As soon as I asked Tommy to slow into a trot, he did, and he followed up with the walk when I asked for that as well.

After that ride, I began taking my newfound trust into the other areas of my life. I knew that what I had accomplished during the trail ride with Tommy was really about trusting myself. The more I built up my own trust, the more I could move into greater success in love and work. This was my current challenge in my spiritual growth. My own trust would help me discern who was worthy of it, but I could only do this if I had enough of it. The lack of trust within causes confusion and uncertainty in the decision-making process, leading to procrastination or unwise choices.

I knew this was a work in progress, but I was beginning to see some fruit from my labor with all I had learned through the chores and energy work at the farm. I began to feel hopeful that the time to quit my job would come soon enough, even if I didn't yet know how I'd make a living. I also felt the twinges of a knowing that my significant other was on his way to me. I was now enthusiastic about beginning to trust and utilize my intuitive abilities as I began my work at the horse rescue in Orange County.

HENRY AND MIDNIGHT
Healing is a Choice

Susie, the owner of the horse rescue, decided she was only interested in my intuitive and energy work services, and did not need me for the horse caretaking. She had many volunteers helping with the caretaking already, but no one who could help the animals heal. Thrilled by the opportunity, I jumped right in.

The first animal I did energy work with at the rescue was a horse named Henry. He was a large-boned, light gray Andalusian, with thinning hair and low energy. On first glance, he looked depressed, as if he had given up on his already long life. Susie told me that he had lived a hardworking life, spending most of his days serving on ranches and farms. His last owner had a trail riding business, and Henry spent many days providing rides in the mountains. Standing next to him, I felt the now familiar feeling of words from another coming into my mind. He said, "Put your hands on me."

I easily placed both of my hands on his back, where I felt intuitively guided. As I did, I felt tingling and warmth in my hands as volumes of heavy energy were released out of this area of his body. I moved my hands along his spine to where I was drawn—across his withers, near his poll, and down to his sacrum.

He snorted and grunted with pleasure the whole time, closing his eyes and holding completely still. I stood there for a long time, feeling the heavy energy leave his physical body through my hands. I heard another voice this time, sounding unlike the animals' voices I'd heard up until this point. It reminded me of a friend or guardian. It said, "You could be here all day." I took this as advice and stopped after awhile.

I would follow up on Henry later, but for now I wanted to move on and see who else I could help. Susie asked me if I would talk to a horse named Midnight. She was a special, mysterious one. Susie wanted to know if she had any requests or desires, or if she wanted to tell us where she came from. No one knew her background.

Before I walked up to Midnight's paddock, I cleared all the lingering energies from Henry's session, grounding and centering myself in preparation for this new one. When I approached her, Midnight, as dark-colored as her name, took one look at me and turned away. Like a human who didn't want to talk, she quickly retreated to the far area of her paddock. I knew she was rejecting me but I didn't take it personally. I could sense Midnight's trust in humans had been betrayed.

I asked her what was wrong, but I got no reply, no words in my head. I did a full self-awareness check-in, tuning in to myself first to know where I was at, and then turned to face her. When I did this, I could feel punches of energy in my solar plexus and heart chakras. It felt like a swirling pressure in both areas, uncomfortable in intensity and slightly nauseating. Unsure of what to make of it, I consulted my Divine Self. I got a feeling of disempowerment in the solar plexus and heartbreak in the heart chakra. Something devastating had happened to this horse. I asked Midnight, "What is it? What happened?"

Unexpectedly, she turned around and made full eye contact for just a brief moment. That one look told me everything. I saw the pictures in my head. At first I saw a middle-aged man wearing blue jeans and a cowboy hat, wielding his rope above his head. Then I saw him riding a horse. A closer look revealed he was riding Midnight. She had a look of despair and despondence in her eyes, like she had fully surrendered to the situation. The man was roping cows while riding Midnight. I had the feeling he went on doing this for hours of the day. Midnight appeared exhausted and oppressed. I knew she had dissociated from her body, because although I saw her body, I could not feel her energy.

When the vision ended and I readjusted myself back to reality, Midnight was standing face-to-face with me at the fence. Anger permeated her being. She seemed to be saying, "There. Are you happy now? Now you know what happened."

I looked back at her, dismayed. "You can heal," I said. "Let me help you release this so you can move on with your life."

"No!"

With that, she retreated again to the back of her paddock. And that was it. There was no more getting her to talk to me.

The voices of the friends and guardians from earlier in the day came back into my head. They explained that she was just not ready to heal. Although I only saw a glimpse of her reality, what she lived through seemed like rape for a human. Midnight had been completely dominated by her rider. She was angry and hurt. She needed time to be ready to heal.

I went to see Susie in her office to discuss the session with Midnight. I asked Susie if Midnight had been a cow horse. I went on to describe the information I received about her being disempowered and heartbroken, and what had happened with her rider. Susie covered her eyes and cried. I stood there confused, not understanding why her sorrow seemed so personal with Midnight.

Susie explained to me that she did in fact know the horse's background. Midnight was her sister's horse. Her sister had put

Midnight in training with a man who was highly recommended and also a cow horse competitor. When her horse came home after weeks of training, she knew something was wrong. Midnight seemed depressed and quieter than usual. Not knowing what else to do, Susie's sister turned to her for help. Susie thought if Midnight spent time with the other horses at the rescue, in a more natural setting, she would begin to heal. Susie apologized for not being upfront about Midnight's history, saying she only wanted me to start off objective, completely open-minded. With that said, she was highly impressed with my abilities.

After taking in everything she had told me, I explained to Susie that, unfortunately, Midnight had for the most part rejected my presence. She did not want to receive healing from a human right now. I suggested she go back to live with Susie's sister, and that maybe her home would provide enough familiarity and comfort to allow her to begin her healing process. It was becoming very clear in my learning as a healer that we can never influence another being to heal through our will. It is their choice when, how, and to what degree they wish to heal.

Although Midnight's situation was a sad one, I knew there would come a day when she would heal. I left the rescue feeling uplifted and confident by the accuracy and advancement of my intuitive abilities. I was certainly learning to trust myself more, being available for whatever information needed to come through. I got a call from Susie later that evening. She told me Henry was doing great. He was running and playing with the other horses in the pasture, and seemed more energetic than ever before. She thanked me for my help that day, and said she looked forward to working with me more.

CHAPTER SEVEN

THE POWER OF HORSE EXPERIENCE

Over the course of the next several months, I took classes for expanding intuitive abilities and learning new energy healing modalities to supplement and better utilize the abilities I was born with. Because I had natural gifts and talents, developed over lifetimes of experience in the intuitive and healing fields, I moved along very quickly in the beginning stages of my career as a healer. I continued sessions with Renée, and volunteered at the farm and horse rescue. I was amazed at the speed with which I was letting go of my fear and self-doubt, and how many positive results I was seeing. Many of the animals at both places continued to improve in overall health and well-being.

I had even been given the chance to work with some goats and sheep that were dying of sepsis. In the process of allowing the healing energies to move through me, using many of the energy protocols I had learned, many of the animals took an immediate turn for the better—in just a few hours. When I went deep inside, I heard the voice of friends in my mind say, "It was their choice. They were on the fence in deciding whether to stay in this lifetime, or pass on and come back again." I trusted all was well.

So much was happening so fast as I was starting to become aware of who these guardians and helpers in my mind were. It sounded a lot like my own thoughts, but slightly different, with a distinct tone, always certain and positive in nature. I discovered these friends were what many call spirit guides. These guides were helping me with the healing work I was doing, as well as directing me in my life. I willingly accepted their advice as long as it resonated with the truth I felt inside of me. So far it had, and I was grateful for their continual, optimistic support. I spent time each day in meditation, connecting to my guides on a deeper level, and asking them to come increasingly closer, so that I could hear them more clearly, see them, and feel even more of their presence.

One morning while meditating, I had a vision of the dream horses, along with the feeling, tone, and energy that always accompanied them in my dreams. I realized that they were guiding me as well, and had been for as long as I'd begun this journey with horses. Although similar to what Linda Kohanov described as the horse ancestors in *The Tao of Equus*, my dream horses are a team of horse spirits who send me information about horses and direct me on my path in helping animals and humans. Through them I have the ability to access the collective horse consciousness. I was excited about having finally discovered the identity of these mysterious beings, and looked forward to increasing my connection and communication with them.

I was still riding whenever I could, and learning greatly from the experiences with Tommy. Most of the time I rode alone, but one day a friend from out of town came to visit. Jenny was someone I had known while living in the Midwest, where we had worked together as nurses.

We had stayed in contact only sporadically through phone and email after I moved to California. When Jenny found out I was riding and working with horses, she was excited to reconnect.

She had always loved horses, spending time riding them off and on as a child. Jenny is a kind, gentle soul, soft-spoken in nature, never wanting to ruffle any feathers. I always enjoyed being around her peaceful, amicable energy, especially in a crazy, chaotic place like a hospital. Outside of work, Jenny was someone I could easily talk to about anything. Her support was steadfast.

We planned to meet at the ranch the first morning after she got in, eager to get on the trails. I asked Katherine if there was another horse she would be willing to let Jenny ride while she was here. Since Jenny wasn't a new rider, and because we'd only be on the trails at the walk or trot, she let me borrow Sheridan.

Sheridan was a mild-mannered Quarter Horse mare with white socks, a white snip down her muzzle, and a long, chestnut-colored mane often tied in braids courtesy of the girls who rode her. When I met her, she reminded me of Jenny quite a bit. She seemed tender, loving, and nurturing on first contact. I learned from Katherine that she had been a dressage horse, and pranced as gracefully as any ballerina. She was also steady and dependable like Tommy, which was why Katherine used her with kids. I thought she would be a perfect match for Jenny. I knew that one way or another, the right horse found the right human, whether the human actually chose them or not. It was by the power of the universe, allowing us to learn whatever we needed to in a horse's presence.

TROUBLE WITH TOMMY
Discernment and Energetic Integrity

Before we went on the trail, I warmed up with Tommy in the arena. He was in a particularly ornery mood—resisting everything I asked of him from the moment I took him out of his stall that morning. I had to wait ten minutes to even get the halter on, and then I had to practically drag him by the lead rope to the arena. What was wrong with him today?

Tommy wouldn't look me in the eye. He seemed completely fixated on the mare and filly nearby. They were running and playing in their paddock together, an extra large-sized living space to account for the two of them. Whatever they were doing, it must have seemed inviting to Tommy. As he locked his feet in place and stared off into the distance, I knew I was in for a challenge.

Finally I got him to pay attention to me, at least for a while. We circled the arena at a walk, and he easily stopped, turned, and changed directions. Getting him up to a trot wasn't a problem, although he kept a slow pace. I wanted to lope in the arena, not only to warm him up, but because I enjoyed it and knew we wouldn't be doing it on the trails today. The trail ride was more to connect with and have fun with a longtime friend.

Tommy gave me trouble again. I asked for the lope at least three times and got nothing but a fast trot, and only some of the time. I was feeling frustrated. I had looked forward to a pleasant day with my friend and instead nothing was going easily.

Tommy continued to refuse to give me the lope. I sat on top of him, feeling defeated and flustered by the whole situation. I knew he wasn't interested. I knew he would probably rather play with the mare and filly nearby. But couldn't he be a little more cooperative here? Couldn't he compromise and give me at least one loping stride? Then we'd be off to a relaxing trail ride. He never opposed that before.

Well, I had it. I lost my common sense. I would not take no for an answer. In this state of insanity I half-jokingly told him we were going to lope right now, right here or I would get the spurs. Filled with embarrassment and guilt immediately after saying it, I saw it had captured his attention. He turned his head slowly towards me and his ears turned around fully, tuning in to my body.

On this note, I grabbed the reins, took a deep breath to energize myself, and asked for the lope. He moved into a fast trot and then changed over quickly into a strong, fast lope. Before I fully integrated what had happened, we were on our second round of the arena, at the same brisk pace. Fully satisfied, I asked him to slow down. Instead, he picked up his stride.

Befuddled, I clung to the saddle while he moved forward at lightning speed. I asked for a lope, and boy, did I get one! He did not seem to get the message to slow down. As I asked him to slow again and again by trying to relax my body and voice, sitting back in my seat as much as I could and bringing the reins in, I got no response. He was still speeding ahead. Tommy clearly was not listening to me. Now I was scared! All I could do was hold on, trying to keep myself in the saddle, hoping I would not fall off but knowing I might, while praying that he would slow down into a slower lope or a jog. Eventually he did. I lost my helmet and my wits, but at least I was safe.

We both breathed laboriously together at the fence when it was over. I slowly got off of him. It took me at least ten minutes to get my bearings and make sense of what had transpired. I looked into Tommy's face and saw the hurt reflected back at me. I also saw regret. I apologized to him. I would not insist he do what he obviously did not want to do today. I would never threaten him with spurs again.

I could now understand and relate to why other humans forced their horses to do what they wanted, even at their own or their horse's expense. It was selfishness, plain and simple. Although Tommy was a strong and opinionated horse, he was normally cooperative and willing when it came to riding. I knew that this wasn't about him having his way with me, but simply a day he didn't feel up to riding, especially in the arena. I had always known how much more he enjoyed the trails rather than arena work.

If this had been another horse who regularly refused certain activities or gaits, I would have come to a different conclusion. Some horses become barn sour, which is a condition that develops because they are kept in a barn, stall, or small paddock for many hours on most days. When it's time to come out and get exercise, play, or work, they often resist or refuse.

In cases like this, it takes time and energy on their human's part to reintroduce the horse to their normal activities. Patiently and persistently, the human must continue to work with the horse, asking him to cooperate until he does willingly. It is essential that the human remain balanced in his use of power, and not use force in the process. Otherwise, the horse might do as he is told, but develop fear and mistrust of the human.

In many of these cases, it might be best to start over with training, and go back to ground work skills and re-establishing the horse-human bond until a horse willingly follows his human's lead again. This is when a human's empowerment is truly evident. Ultimately, it is the human's responsibility to make sure the horse gets the optimum amount of time spent doing his everyday activities, which can prevent him from becoming barn sour. Unfortunately, in our busy, fast-paced culture, many horse owners don't have the time to work with their horses as consistently as they need it. Many horses are lucky to even get the necessary basic care and attention on a daily basis.

Because of the power struggles humans and horses can get into, it is important to be conscientious and discerning when determining the cause behind a horse's lack of cooperation during activities. We must ask pertinent questions. Is the horse feeling unwell or having pain, is he scared or resistant because of a change in his usual environment, or is he simply bored?

We especially need to consider whether the horse actually enjoys the same activities we do. If not, we need to make a change in our activity repertoire, or consider finding the horse a human who is a better match. As I said earlier, a true partnership between horse and human means both species' needs and desires are considered and honored. A relationship is never one-sided. Sometimes a compromise needs to be made. Sometimes we need to take the time to offer safety and tenderness if a horse is adjusting to something new.

As Chris Irwin explained in his book *Horses Don't Lie*, assertive behavior, with a take-charge attitude, will make it easier for you to be the leader in the herd of you and your horse. Our horses should never push us around or control us. But this does not mean that it's appropriate to be a tyrant, lashing out at them with anger and rage when they don't do what we ask. They are negatively impacted by these emotions just the same as our friends, family, and neighbors are.

As Adele, Marlena, and Thomas McCormick explained in *Horses and the Mystical Path*, being combative never helps you acquire leadership. It is far more effective to build up your inner strength, self-esteem and willpower, creating a deeper bond and long-lasting friendship with your horse in the process. The improved self-esteem and empowerment you achieve through your personal growth and continual horse experience, gained both on the ground and with riding, will help you become more confident and better able to step into a leadership role.

A dominant horse who repeatedly gives you trouble—by taking off with you or bucking without warning, for example—needs extra training and ground work, especially if you are fully aware of and processing your emotions when these behaviors occur. Consult or hire a horse trainer for further feedback and guidance with these issues. Engage in basic horsemanship activities such as grooming, leading, walking with your horse at liberty, hanging out together in their turn-out or pasture area without an agenda, and playing bonding games like the horse dance with Percy I described in Chapter One. These activities keep the relationship strong, which will ensure your horse respects you, honors your safety, and considers your needs as much as their own.

If you intend to ride a horse that is not yours, make sure to spend ample time with them before you ever go on a single ride. During at least the first two meetings, participate in the basic horsemanship activities I discussed above. Practice sending and receiving telepathic messages (see Chapter Twelve for how to communicate with animals), so you can get a better idea of the horse's interests, preferences, temperament, and current emotional state.

In addition, follow your intuition and avoid intimate activities with a horse that you feel uneasy or anxious around. Sometimes two clashing personalities attempting to unite in a shared activity can be a dangerous combination that can cause accidents. In many cases, the differences between horse and human can be worked out, just as they can between humans, but I would recommend that you participate in horsemanship activities or get training together first, before you test things out on a ride.

Keep in mind the old saying, "It takes two to tango." Any riding problem is a warning that there is something going on with you *and* the horse, so take a look at both sides of the story to find the causes and solutions. The goal is to promote a healthy partnership, one where you lead, but also consider and cooperate with the horse's needs, desires, and ideas under specific circumstances—circumstances that bring about the greatest good for both of you.

Unfortunately, many who might have witnessed what I went through while riding Tommy could think that I looked and sounded like an empowered leader in the beginning. I was strong and determined enough to get him—a thousand-pound animal—to follow my command, through my words, body, and energy. A human might begin to believe that if I could do that, I could make anything happen.

But I had to consider the cost. Although I didn't use physical force (or even get the spurs), I was frustrated and angry, and I unleashed this energy on him. I also threatened to use spurs on him, and since others had used spurs while riding Tommy, he took me seriously. The energy behind my words and the mention of spurs were associated with control and domination in Tommy's mind. This energetic domination, although different from physical domination, which involves the use of physical force with tools, is not empowerment. In this case, since Tommy was clearly not up to loping in the arena, it would have been better to try another day or work on the ground with him until he was ready or willing to follow my leadership again.

Standing there, reflecting on the incident, I had another epiphany. I recalled the moment I became startled by his second round of the arena at the lope. I had not continually asked for the lope with my body or energy, like I normally need to do. Knowing how sensitive he is, I realized he must have felt the fearful energy running through me; his bolting off even faster was his response. The faster he went, the more my fear increased, which led to more speed. He was simply reacting to my energy. I was now so relieved that neither of us had been injured in this vicious cycle!

After taking the time to soothe and comfort each other, like a couple after an argument, I decided to let him spend some time doing what he really wanted to do today. Neither species can work all the time; we all need time to goof off. I led him into the paddock next to the mare and her filly. Immediately, they connected over the fence, neighing and grooming each other, mirroring one another as they ran parallel along the fence, playing their own games. Play is just as important for wellness in horses as it is in humans.

JENNY AND SHERIDAN
Healing Sexual Abuse

Eventually I tore myself away from Tommy's stall—spontaneously deciding to let him have the day off. I went over to the stall of a gentle Draft gelding named Max. Max was like a sweet but giant teddy bear who was always excited to get out on the trails. As I got him ready, I found Jenny waiting at the end of the ranch. She had arrived and been introduced to Sheridan by Katherine. In just a short period of time, we were saddled up and off to the trails.

Sheridan and Max seemed to get along amiably, as gelding and mare. They easily switched leads when one felt energetic or needed a break. It was a calm and tranquil ride in the midday California desert sun. Jenny and I talked, catching up on everything that had gone on in our lives since we last connected. My life was the usual tale of ups and downs, trials and accomplishments—including all my goals in sight, yet to be met. Max skipped along effortlessly as I explained where I was at, and where I still needed to go in life.

At first when Jenny spoke, Sheridan seemed content. She walked on in her steady, easy-going stride. Jenny said everything in her life was fine. She was still working as a nurse in Wisconsin. She and her husband were trying to have kids. She said she felt the time was right. They had always wanted children, were well into their thirties, their jobs and health were stable, and financially they were thriving. But when Jenny finished her sentence, I noticed Sheridan start to pick up the pace. It didn't seem to be related to her wanting to catch up to Max. She skipped and slowed, skipped and slowed, as if responding to something.

Jenny asked Sheridan to walk, and she did—temporarily. But then as she went back to the kid discussion, Sheridan went back to the trotting. It almost seemed to be a repeat of the morning

I had with Tommy, but this was a different dynamic altogether. Jenny was not feeling afraid or frustrated while riding Sheridan. It had something to do with her feelings about having kids. Finally, Jenny stopped talking and just let Sheridan trot forward for a while. I followed behind her on Max, unsure of what was going on. After I caught up to them, I saw Jenny was crying. "What's wrong?" I asked.

What came out of Jenny's mouth next was something I would have never expected.

She blurted it all out. "I hate this. I have always hated it."

Confused, I asked, "What?"

"I have always been uncomfortable with how a horse feels underneath me. I have never liked the movement of the horse."

I sat back in the saddle, trying to make sense of what she told me. "Is it painful physically, or are you afraid you'll fall off?" I could tell Jenny knew exactly what it was.

"No." Tears streamed down her face as she continued to ride on. "This is why we can't have kids."

"Wait…stop. Stop the horse."

Clearly the riding was disturbing her deeply. I had to talk to her about what was going on here. I didn't want our time spent together to be like this. Maybe it had just been a really long time since she had been on a horse.

We stopped near a bench overlooking a beautiful swimming hole and tied the horses to a couple trees nearby. As we sat down, Jenny began to explain. She and her husband were trying to have kids, but she did not enjoy sex. She never had, just as she had never enjoyed riding a horse faster than at a walk, even though she loved horses. The movement was too bouncy, and she was uncomfortable with the intensity between her legs.

She always felt awkward and embarrassed by it—having a horse between her legs. And it was because of these intense feelings in her body that sex with her husband did not go smoothly.

Most of the time, they would either have to stop completely or she would shut down to get through it. At least when she checked out, they could complete the deed, and try to make a baby. Jenny also wanted her husband to get his needs met some of the time. These sexual issues had been worsening for her over the last two years.

Astounded, I sat there and tried to make sense of it. All of this, in just the first twenty minutes of a trail ride? And to think it all came out because of Sheridan's trotting. Or was Sheridan's trotting a result of Jenny's physical and emotional baggage? I couldn't help but ask Jenny if she had ever been sexually abused.

I knew from both personal experience and from the EFL training that riding can often bring up sexual issues in women. It is a combination of the physical sensations of having a horse between your legs—the rubbing of certain parts of the genitalia if you are positioned correctly on the horse—as well as the movement of the horse that simulates the act of sex.

This is particularly acute for women who have been abused. With riding, some who had totally repressed the experience might have flashes of old, buried memories of the abuse; while others who have always known could be reminded again. In either case, riding can definitely be a trigger for the bodily trauma and emotional and mental agony associated with the assaults, and any other experience of being victimized.

Jenny said that, as far as she knew, she was not abused in this way, but she was starting to question it. Why in the world would she not enjoy sex, one of life's greatest pleasures?

I told her that from my studies in psychology and the clinical work I'd done since then, I discovered that many people don't remember sexual abuse as a child, and sometimes even sexual assaults that happen as an adult. In many cases, the memories, emotions, and all other sensations associated with the trauma are suppressed or repressed as a survival mechanism. A reality that is too much to bear could otherwise break a fragile ego, causing severe mental illness such as psychosis.

Unfortunately, as the book *Soul Retrieval: Mending the Fragmented Self* by Sandra Ingerman summed up, when one experiences enough trauma to overwhelm the psyche, often there is soul loss. The person is then left with an emptiness, a fragmented self that is wounded and unfulfilled, always searching in others and the world for those missing links to bring back security, safety, and wholeness. From other research on the topic, including Ellen Bass and Laura Davis's book *The Courage to Heal: A Guide For Women Survivors of Child Sexual Abuse*, I learned that those who think it might have happened usually can confirm it later through memories, flashbacks, and/or dreams. When I say they remember, I mean that the memories come in vividly through thoughts, bodily sensations, images, and through the other senses (smell, sound, taste, touch, etc.), usually at a time in their life when they have acquired enough physical safety and emotional strength to handle it.

The good news is that many people who have been sexually assaulted, whether or not they remember it, can naturally heal these wounds through riding. Children especially, with their open, unguarded energy, can heal easily this way. The trauma is released and the triggers are often worked through unknowingly. Surprised to hear this, Jenny asked me to tell her more.

I explained that horseback riding can help you heal for a couple reasons. First, it is a horse and riding, not a human and sex, so you are not repeating exactly the same thing within the same species, and are therefore less likely to have a full-blown reaction if triggered by an old memory. Horseback riding—because of the movements and degree of sensuality involved—is similar enough to sex to get the attention of your unconscious, and it is productive to have it worked out in a situation where you are in charge, without worrying about anyone else's needs not being met or feelings being hurt, including your own in such an intimate encounter. The horse will not take offense to how many times you start, stop, and even get off and take a break!

Many people who are sexually abused choose sexual partners who have a similar vibration as the person who abused them. This is due to an unconscious attempt to heal the original trauma, what Sigmund Freud called *repetition compulsion*.[1] This is another reason why people who are unconscious of the abuse keep experiencing the same trauma over and over again, in the choice of partners who are abusive or who carry a predator-like energy, engaging in such activities as voyeurism, exhibitionism, and an interest in pornography. If the abuse is worked through on all levels of one's being, they will no longer be drawn to an abusive vibration, and will instead choose a healthy partner.

So, how does the healing happen? I went on to explain it to Jenny. The connection usually begins on the ground first. This happens frequently with those who synchronistically run into or buy a horse they feel immediately drawn to. There is often a spiritual agreement between yourself and a particular horse, that you will help each other heal and grow. A lot of healing can occur in the beginning, just through feeling your emotions in the safe presence of unconditional love and compassion, and commonly, in the mirror of resonance shown before you in the horse.

Grooming, bathing, hoof picking, and leading are ways to deepen the connection between you and your horse through the physical contact. This is essential in the healing process. Always be completely present with a horse in his or her stall or pasture. I recommend doing the self-awareness check-in if you know or think you might have a history of any kind of physical or sexual trauma. Be aware of what you are feeling during every moment you spend with your horse, so you and your horse remain grounded and safe. If you feel drawn to riding, or have already been doing so, remember to do the self-awareness check-in before each ride.

IMPORTANT: Do not attempt to work with horses, whether on the ground or in the saddle, to assist in healing without the help of a facilitator of Equine Facilitated Psychotherapy (EFP), Equine Assisted Psychotherapy (EAP), Equine Facilitated Mental Health (EFMH), or another experienced equine therapy practitioner who has background and training in helping those with trauma and abuse issues. This is especially true if you have a psychiatric history—including drug or alcohol abuse, eating disorders, or self-mutilation—or if you have difficulty processing emotions or become unable to function well in daily living while experiencing intense emotions. EFL work should not be a substitute for treatment of physical or mental/emotional health issues with a licensed medical professional.

Do not attempt to learn how to ride with a healing intention by yourself. This can lead to accidents and trauma for both human and horse. An EFP, EAP, or EFMH practitioner who is also a riding instructor can help you in this healing process. They will also be able to verify if the horse is willing and able to help you heal. For a list of qualified equine therapy professionals who are also riding instructors, contact the Professional Association of Therapeutic Horsemanship International (PATH Intl.), formerly the North American Riding for the Handicapped Association (NARHA), at (800) 369-RIDE or www.pathintl.org.

As Adele, Marlena, and Thomas McCormick shared in their books, and as most facilitators of horse healing work know, some horses have no interest in helping humans in this area. If we insist upon their service, they can be traumatized by being coerced into a role as a counselor, which includes the task of maintaining their presence while being exposed to our darkest emotions. This can lead to emotional flooding, fear, helplessness, and loss of self-worth due to their lack of control. If we were in their hooves, we'd want to have a choice in the matter. This is why it is paramount that we accurately discern and honor whether they truly wish to do emotional work with us (and that we are not projecting our own desire onto them).

In any case, because all humans have had some kind of trauma in their lives, if you enjoy riding, be aware that uncomfortable physical sensations, thoughts, or emotions can arise spontaneously. It is important to know that this can happen to anyone who rides, because of horses' natural ability to help us heal. If or when you become aware of these feelings and thoughts, stop the horse. It might help to express how you are feeling in the moment with the horse. Breathe. If the emotions or physical sensations arise again, stop the horse again, or get off the horse and take a break. If you receive disturbing images, are no longer able to stay focused, or become overwhelmed in any way, stop riding, and seek help from a licensed medical professional.

After Jenny and I talked, she told me she thought she experienced some healing with Sheridan today. She was also inspired to get back into riding again at home. There was a riding facility nearby, and I gave her a contact number of a facilitator of EFP in her area. She was glad to have extra resources available to help her, and was grateful for the illuminating experience she had with Sheridan and me. She had never consciously admitted to problems in her sex life before. Jenny now knew that it was important that she talk to her husband about possibly seeing a marriage therapist for extra support.

The trail ride back to the ranch was graceful and lighthearted, and we ended the day together with a nice dinner. It felt good to share with Jenny in the way we did, and our friendship was deepened in the process. When she left that night, we promised to stay in touch like always. I looked forward to hearing how things would begin to change in her life and marriage.

JUDY AND ROYAL
Authenticity and Boundaries

Over the next two years, I continued to gain experience in EFL, and with my own intuitive-healing work. I was already doing some readings and healings for pay, but I now desired to expand my practice. In the beginning, many of my referrals came from one of the horse rescues where I had volunteered. I also put up flyers around town and set up a page on a local healing service website.

One of my first paying customers was a horse-human duo client, Judy and Royal. Judy was in her mid-fifties at the time. She considered herself a retired horsewoman, although she was still doing trail riding and ground work with her horse. Royal was a flea-bitten Quarter Horse she had owned for over fifteen years.

Judy first began learning to ride with Royal at age forty. Then within five years she began participating in hunter-jumper and dressage shows. She trained and worked hard in this area for almost ten years. Judy and Royal enjoyed it, but it was also stressful for both of them. Judy became competitive, and she pushed Royal and herself very hard to win. In the process, she developed confidence in herself—not only with riding but also with every area of her life. Since childhood she had been a shy, insecure person who thought she was never capable of anything. Her mother had often instilled this belief in her by telling her a woman's purpose was only to raise children. Judy was also not a very good student and didn't have many friends. This followed her into her adult life, so when she found she had talent with riding, she stuck to it, determined to be successful in something. And she was. As she began winning shows, she began winning friends, and even got married. This was another first for her, because she never had success with men in the past.

But there was a cost to all the competition. Royal often suffered careless injuries that Judy now suspected were a result of
too much work. At the time, she didn't see any correlation between the competition and his injuries. In fact, the more Royal
needed to rest, the harder she pushed him to work. She thought
it was right to have control over her horse. The trainers she hired
had told her that letting him slack off or giving him an excuse to
achieve less than perfection would only give Royal a reason to be
unmotivated. During this whole period of time in her life, she
thought she was just being a good horsewoman. Knowledgeable
and more experienced horse people modeled strict routine and
tough manners and the more she followed their lead, the better
she felt about herself.

It was finally when Royal developed a near fatal bout of colic
that the truth hit her. All that mattered to Judy was that he got
better. She promised him the strict schedules and shows would
stop if he wanted, anything that would help him get and stay
better. Miraculously, he improved. Judy decided they had enough
blue ribbons and excitement, so they slowed down. They became
trail-riding companions.

Royal's uplifted mood and improving health seemed to show
he was happy with that. Judy also realized that much of what she
thought was her pride and self-worth with her hard work was a
façade. Although she gained confidence in herself through riding,
her true self-worth and self-respect came through her relationship
with Royal. His loyalty and love for her never wavered throughout
his injuries and illness. Obviously, it was about who she was deep
down, not what she accomplished on a physical level that made
her okay—even better than okay. How about wonderful? Royal
seemed to think so, and their bond became more intimate in the
time they spent together after his illness.

But now they were having trouble again. Royal was acting
more and more tired and withdrawn. He began to pull away

from her when she would come down to his barn to visit with him or groom him. On days she wanted to ride, he would often object—pulling back from the tack and lowering his head in the process. She knew he was not interested, but was not sure why. She wondered if he was sick again, but thought it was unlikely because he was eating, drinking, and eliminating well.

When I checked in with Royal, I did not sense anything going on with him physically. I did notice that he was depressed and anxious. I told Judy I wanted to observe how she interacted with him. I led Judy through the self-awareness check-in. A wobbly and fidgety Judy walked in the round pen to greet her beloved and immediately, he reared straight up in the air. Even after her self-awareness check-in, he was still picking up on something unknown to Judy. I asked her to pay attention to the sensations she noted before going in, but she kept saying she was fine, that she could barely feel them now. She stepped forward to reach out to Royal. He bucked and kicked out, then ran off in the opposite direction. Worried about her safety and realizing that she was not really tuning in to her body, I asked her to step out of the round pen so we could talk.

I pointed out two things. First of all, she was not being genuine. Horses, because of their instinctual prey nature, are always aware of how we are really feeling in the moment. This is how they know whether they are safe or not in our presence. Horses do this in the wild when they assess by his energy whether a lion or bear has recently eaten or not, thus knowing when to continue grazing or move on to avoid an attack. As I discussed previously in Chapter Four, if you are incongruent, and your body language does not match your emotions and energy, horses will become stressed, uncomfortable, and untrusting.

I explained this to Judy and asked her to truly check in with her body and how she was feeling. This time when she did, she told me about a few dull sensations she felt in her chest and solar plexus. She could not access any emotions related to them, but at least she was more aware of her body. I asked her what was currently going on in her life. While she had been in the round pen, I communicated with Royal. He showed me a picture of Judy bent over the kitchen table, crying. She explained that her husband had been emotionally abusive over the course of their marriage, and that just a couple weeks ago, he announced out of the blue that he was leaving her—that he simply did not love her anymore. I looked at Judy while she spoke and did not see any emotions emerge in her physical exterior, even though this huge, traumatic life event had just occurred.

I described the second thing I had noticed while she was in the round pen with Royal. Royal was setting boundaries with her, and she had not respected them. Boundaries, for humans and horses, allow us to set limits for establishing safety and comfort. As Wyatt Webb shared in *It's Not About the Horse*, horses attempt to set boundaries through their non-verbals and body language, such as moving away from us when we approach. If this is not honored, they will become distressed and may act out with unpleasant behaviors, like rearing up, bucking, and kicking. This is what happened with Judy and Royal. Instead of respecting his need for space, shown by his moving away in response to her energy, Judy pushed forward and tried to touch him. Royal became angered by this, and he bucked and kicked in response to his feelings—demanding his space. I explained to Judy that often horses act out what we are not aware of in ourselves or our relationships. Perhaps he was picking up on a boundary that was never upheld between Judy and her husband?

Judy explained that she was not respecting boundaries in many of her relationships lately. She was feeling so needy and desperate, she was calling friends at all hours of the night, dropping by uninvited, and had even asked a friend if she could move in this week. She received many of these same responses—irritation, aggravation, and ultimately rejection, just like with Royal. This only made it worse, and she felt even more needy.

We took some time to talk about this outside the round pen—the fear, anger, pain, and suffering she had gone through in her dysfunctional marriage, the sense of betrayal and depression she had buried about her husband not loving her anymore, all of which was more than likely leading to Royal's recent withdrawn behavior and demeanor. I spent time helping her process the shock of the sudden end to her marriage. No wonder Royal had gotten worse again over the last couple weeks. He was refusing to interact with her in any way until she became aware of what was happening inside of her!

After taking some time to be with all of this, Judy's eyes teared up. She eventually went in the round pen again, spending a few moments with Royal. This time he came right up to her, and gently nuzzled his face against her chest. She remained in the present moment the whole time, breathing, and being aware of the sensations in her body. I reminded her to not think ahead or plan, but to just be aware of what was happening right now, between her and Royal.

When she exited the round pen, Judy appeared, by her strong, steady body movements and relaxed energy, calmer and grounded. She told me she felt more safe and sure of herself now than she had felt over the last few weeks. Her husband had already left. She now knew she needed to spend some time alone, just being with herself and her feelings for at least the next week. She would call her sister and make some kind of long-term plan when she had time to think things over. I recommended a good therapist that she could begin to work with.

I followed up with Judy a couple weeks later and found that things were improving for her and Royal. The night after the session, she cried herself to sleep. She spent the whole next day outside with Royal, just sitting with him in his turnout area. He was easily responding and interacting with her. Judy knew she could ride him now, but was simply content to just be with him.

She continued to process the feelings about her husband's abuse—the name-calling, controlling, the manipulation of her schedule and her life—and the loss of him. She made an appointment with the therapist I recommended, so she could gain additional support while developing a greater sense of stability in her life. She was already beginning to feel a sense of relief financially, because her sister offered her a place to stay if she needed it while she sorted things out with her husband in the separation.

This session was another immense validation for the value of this work, proving how a major shift like this could occur for a human and their horse, simply by being aware of one's feelings, becoming more authentic through feeling them, and learning to set and honor healthy boundaries.

As the many stories in Chapters Five and Six exemplified, horses help us begin, move through, and complete a healing process. We start by being held in a safe container of unconditional love, which allows us to get in touch with our deepest fears, grief, physical pain, illness, and suffering. If we are unable to recognize or take full responsibility for our health and well-being, our horses will show us what is going on with us on a mental, emotional, physical, or behavioral level through their empathic reactions. As we work and spend time with what is going on inside of us, as in the cases of the previous stories, the horses will help us energetically release what no longer serves us.

As this chapter illuminated, horses also teach us how to overcome fear, insecurity, self-doubt, and sexual issues, which leads to a greater level of confidence, trust, boundaries, and compassion. They help us develop self-love and self-respect, and a powerful sense of our own worthiness, attracting the same in all of our relationships.

As we master these qualities individually, we carry them on an energetic level—emitting them in our world and helping every living being we have contact with through our example.

CHAPTER EIGHT

WILD HORSE LESSONS FOR HUMANITY

So far in this book I have explored the life hardships, needs, desires, and teaching and healing capacities of domestic horses. These are the horses that we tend to have regular contact with in our everyday lives. But what about the wild horses? While providing my healing services to some horses that were taken from the wild, and from my research and the information I received from the horse spirits, I discovered that these amazing beings are the essence of freedom and power in our world. Wild horses play an immense role in helping us further our spiritual growth and evolution, individually and as a whole.

Wild horse herds and bands are a great model for healthy human family systems. I am always blown away by the spiritual mastery of their collective. They naturally portray community, with each individual working as part of a team. Although there is a natural pecking order or levels of hierarchy within the wild herd, each member is valued for the role they fill in the group. They all work together for the greatest good of the whole.

This is very different from our human culture, where the old, less attractive, or physically disabled are often unacknowledged, abused, or abandoned by society. Why is it that we don't recognize the wisdom that elders bring, or the unique gifts and compassion that the physically disabled or weak can offer to our world? In large herds, all members help meet the group need for safety through their numbers. As Carolyn Resnick explained in *Naked Liberty* and Jaime Jackson described in *The Natural Horse: Foundations for Natural Horsemanship*, every horse contributes to the group mind consciousness, allowing the herd to operate as one functional entity.

I have also noticed that wild horses lead differently than humans, and we could benefit from their example. In our current, masculine-dominated society, rationality and force haven't helped us reach the goals of peace and harmony we've been striving for as a group. With horses, the leader is not necessarily the one who is physically stronger, pushy, or active. As Mark Rashid shared in his book *Horses Never Lie: The Heart of Passive Leadership*, they are not the bullies you might find kicking, biting, or tormenting the other horses. These bullies are commonly found in domestic herds and use physical and energetic intimidation to gain the upper hand, to be able to eat and drink first at the feeder, or claim their place first in the barn.

Often you will see the true lead horse standing around the sidelines, completely relaxed and at ease. In this state of being, they can connect to that present awareness within, which leads to great insights and wisdom. A true lead horse, what Rashid called "a passive leader," is always "calm and consistent." Rashid wrote, "Their quiet confidence and lack of force or aggression appears to be something that other horses look for and, when given the opportunity, actively seek out."[1]

Contrary to what is frequently seen in the human culture, the decision-maker and leader, taking her place at the front of the herd, is often female. In the wild, she chooses when, how, and where the herd travels, taking them to appropriate food and water sources. She often achieves this role through power-ful emotional traits such as tenacity and courage, receptivity to group needs, and a keen intuition.

Because she easily takes initiative, and proves herself trust-worthy through practicality, the other horses are naturally in-clined to follow her. As reported by Jaime Jackson, a farrier who studied horses in the wild, in his book *The Natural Horse*, most female-led herds appeared more stable and harmonious. The stallions, believed by many to be the usual leaders, will often be seen picking up the rear in a herd on the move. This reflects their role as protector from predators. In specific herds, there are bachelor bands where stallions will lead, but this is not always the case.

Wild horses also instinctually seek out healing from the earth. They know nothing of the doctors that we find ourselves obsessed with. When out of balance, they go to their original source of health and nourishment. This can be observed in sick or dying animals who go off into the woods or an area of nature hidden from view. They do this to heal, but also to hide from potential predators who are able to spot them when they are out in the open fields or meadows. If they are able to recover, releas-ing whatever was blocking their life-force energies, you will see them reappear when the healing process is complete.

The healing electromagnetic field of earth helps in this pro-cess, naturally clearing heavy energies and promoting healthy body functioning. In particular, the negative ions that horses absorb from water sources and after rains increase cellular re-generation and strengthen the immune system. Furthermore, electrons released from earth's energy field bind to free radicals that could otherwise cause cellular damage and disease. Clinton Ober, Stephen Sinatra, and Martin Zucker discussed this idea more thoroughly in their book *Earthing: The Most Important Health Discovery Ever?* The tender, soothing energy of the earth's surface, experienced through being in direct physical contact, makes it an inviting place to get the rest and relaxation necessary for revitalization of health.

Many horses might also feel drawn to eating certain plants or flowers that grow in the area where they reside, helping to promote the healing process. This explains why many holistic forms of treatment, such as homeopathy, herbs, aromatherapy, or flower essences, help them heal in a way that is complementary to their natural way of living. Wild horses haven't yet been subjected to invasive means of treating illness, such as surgical procedures or the chemicals and synthetic compounds found in drugs or chemotherapy.

One of the most important lessons that humanity can learn from wild and domestic horses is how to embrace our femininity. This is beginning to happen in our world today, as we are living in a time of a great shift in consciousness. This shift affects all levels of our being and our lives, including Mother Earth. We are moving from a society that mainly operates on masculine principles, to one that thrives from utilizing more feminine qualities such as receptivity, caring, nurturing, community, intuition, cooperation, or creativity. Healing our wounds related to the rejection of our innate femininity will not only empower women, but will help men as well. Both men and women carry the opposite sex's energy inside.

When the Tao Master Lao Tsu said, "Know the strength of a man, but keep a woman's care,"[2] he was describing what is natural for horses. They carry the energy of both sexes, but as prey animals, they more frequently utilize their feminine attributes. We are learning that both the feminine and masculine are equally valuable and needed in our lives, but female energy is necessary in areas of leadership right now. Living primarily in a logical, rational, left-brained, systematic way will no longer serve us as a collective, and so we are called to become more heart-centered. As we lead from our hearts, becoming more compassionate and intuitive, we can truly understand and accept unity consciousness.

TRANSCENDING DUALITY IN OUR NEW WORLD

Unity consciousness is based on the idea that all humans, no matter what race, culture, religion, gender, sexual orientation, or economic status, are equal. This goes for all species of the animal and nature kingdom as well. We are all connected, and one person, animal, or aspect of nature affects the greater whole. When we are in balance our well-being affects the greater whole for the better. When we have fully embodied this understanding, and it resonates throughout our being, our example helps others in our world follow suit.

This will bring great peace, harmony, cooperation, and freedom for and between all humans, animals, and living beings on Earth. It will change our lifestyles in a positive way, from how we take care of our health and our environment, to how we use money, to what we choose to do for a living and how much we work. We will begin to take responsibility for our lives, and many of us will finally receive our fair share, flourishing instead of struggling to get by on a day-by-day basis.

In order to get there, we must each individually work on releasing our own personal fears, thereby, through example, helping all in the human collective release the fears that have built up over millions of lifetimes, often due to trauma and hardship. Only after we have substantially overcome our fears will we truly be receptive to the love, beauty, and abundance around us, and be able to make changes that will benefit everyone in the world. Taking these steps forward means being vulnerable. Unfortunately, our understanding of vulnerability has been distorted.

Contrary to common human opinion, vulnerability does not reflect a weakness or suggest that we are setting ourselves up for attack. It is really a place of empowerment. Spiritually speaking, when we are vulnerable, we inherently comprehend, from deep within our core, that we cannot be physically or emotionally injured. Only after a great deal of personal and collective healing can we gain enough spiritual strength, support, and connection to put down our guard because we know it is truly safe. We can then open up to let our authentic souls shine through our human shells.

Wild horses model this vulnerability through their actions. They aren't afraid to be who they are. They radiate innocence, wonder, enchantment, a youthful joy and delight, and authentic emotion in response to what they experience in every moment. Unlike us, they don't have to pretend to be different than who they are in order to survive or fit in with their herd. Fortunately, this is actively changing with humans in our current culture.

Wild horses also utilize creative principles like imagination in their everyday lives. They don't go to sleep worrying about whether an attack from the past will happen again. They start each day fresh and new. They leave behind the past of each day— each moment—completely. Eckhart Tolle shared a great example of this in his book *The New Earth: Awakening to Your Life's Purpose*. After having a squabble, two ducks in the wild release their toxic thoughts and emotions by flapping their wings and splashing in the water. They are then on with their day and into the next moment. Their now neutral beliefs, thoughts, and emotions create each novel experience they have from that moment forward. They make the reality they experience what it is and they imagine it into being through their expectations.

I have found some instances to the contrary. Some wild horses, as well as other wild animals, like those at particular animal sanctuaries, parks, or zoos, are unable to imagine a healthy life into being because they are in constant close proximity to humans who have toxic bodies, minds, and emotions. Many of them become more domesticated in the process, and therefore develop physical, mental, and emotional imbalances similar to ours. On account of their empathic nature, the animals also pick up and absorb the heavy energies around them like a sponge. Although their connection to Earth will help them initially clear the energies, they will often reabsorb them through repeated exposure. This idea is also the rationale for why wild horses are unable to heal physical health disorders caused by continuous contact with chemicals or toxic compounds found in their natural habitats.

On a different note, wild horses—and other wild animals—can teach us how to accept the natural course of the life cycle, because they don't have the attachment to physical form that we have. They don't have anxiety or fear about when their time of death will come, and therefore don't try to fight the process of aging and dying. The emotional stability and peaceful energy that they radiate throughout their dying and death time shows us how to transition more easily and gracefully.

Wild horses also have the ability to help us remember who we truly are at our core. All living beings have a Divine Self or God within. Wild horses, through being in balance with nature, in constant contact with Earth, and one with their families, never lose that spiritual connection, unless they are taken out of their natural habitat. We can pick up on their lead and reconnect with nature, getting back to our biological roots that help us tap into that infinite, wise aspect within. When we do this, it is easier to let go of all false identities and personas. This also helps ease the process of death, because after the transition, only our soul lives on.

Lastly, the wild horses can teach us how to be more comfortable with our sexuality and sensuality. Unfortunately, in our culture, the sexual act is often distorted through inappropriate behaviors and abuse, as with the predation of our children, exhibitionism, and voyeurism. It is also overexposed in the media, and yet it's denied in our family and educational systems; for example, in our common reluctance to instruct our young on the natural desires and body functions, including how to protect themselves from pregnancy or disease. Contrarily, we see the natural, appropriate sexual responses modeled vividly in the explicit way horses mate, give birth, and care for their young. They don't carry the shame we do, and they don't attempt to restrain or repress these natural desires and processes.

I want to emphasize the horses' ability to let their sensual side shine through in their experiences of living. If they have pleasure or pain, the humans and other life forms nearby will witness the beauty in these expressions. We can easily visualize these sensual responses in all wild horses, as we watch them cool off in a creek or river, groan in delight as they eat from nature's bounty, yelp in pain when pushed or kicked by other herd members, or in the sweet, affectionate way a mare grooms her foal. When we glimpse these happenings, we can remember that we too are in a physical body that comes from nature. We are here to be present in these bodies, and to feel all of it—the pleasures and pains. That is one of the many purposes of our incarnations on this planet—to experience what it is like to be a spiritual being in a human body.

The challenge in attaining balance between these two aspects of our being is what we are here on Earth to master. Even though our purpose is to fully experience being in a physical body, we are also here to develop spiritually through expanding our consciousness. Maintaining the connection to our spiritual nature can prevent us from becoming overly absorbed in our physicality. As is easily seen in our world today, when it comes to the value we place on physical beauty, intelligence, and how much we achieve, many humans behave as if they are only physical beings. They are ignorant of the fact that none of these qualities are who they really are, and thereafter their self-worth, confidence, or happiness diminishes.

This is where the wild horses can help us again. They don't live with mirrors like we do, but I'm convinced that even if they did, they would not scowl at what they saw or become depressed or discouraged by a particular physical quality or lack of one. Even though they are a different species, their inherent nature and living style can still influence us for the better, if we let it motivate us.

Honoring the wild horses and allowing them to live naturally, be who they are, and to model all of the above lessons to us—community, leadership, how to heal from Earth, embracing our femininity, creating through the imagination, comfort with sexuality and sensuality, and how to move beyond the physical through connection to our spiritual selves—helps us be happier and healthier, expanding our awareness every step of the way.

Our good health and happiness also influences horses' welfare for the better, which is the basis of unity consciousness, one of the results of the current shift in consciousness for all beings on Earth. As we spiritually evolve, we begin to perceive our relationships with other humans differently, caring more about how our neighbors and community members are doing, not just our close friends and family. We also view our affinity with animals and the nature kingdom in a different way. We learn that we are all in this together, and that every living being's wellness impacts our ability to coexist—to thrive as a whole.

This makes sense when we consider the example of cutting down too many trees and how that decreases oxygen levels in the air, reduces or eliminates natural habitats for animals, and breaks down the maintenance of the ecosystem. Another long-term solution for bringing the ecosystem back into balance is by introducing precise numbers of predator species into specific areas where they have diminished. Hunting, although a pastime cherished by many, is not a successful way to control the overpopulation of prey animals such as horses or deer, according to Mike Cavaroc, wildlife photographer and explorer.

Cavaroc expanded further on this idea in his online article "Why America Needs More Predators."[3] There is a common misconception that reestablishing more predators could threaten human lives. But wildlife predators prefer particular animal species as their prey. Managing proper predator-prey ratios in the wild helps provide stability within the animal portion of the food chain.

In addition to this, the health of many farm animals—such as pigs, cows, or chickens—directly affects us as well, because we consume their meat, milk, and eggs. And so when it comes to horses, we ask the next question: how can we improve and maintain their health?

PART THREE

IMPROVING AND MAINTAINING HEALTH IN OUR HORSES

CHAPTER NINE

U

A HORSE OWNER'S RESPONSIBILITY

After understanding the many ways horses help us heal, we naturally become inspired to help them. They pick up our thoughts, emotions, illnesses, and behavior patterns, taking on the heavy burdens we are not able to shoulder on our own. They offer a great container of healing to us through their unconditional love, compassion, safe presence, groundedness, present-centered awareness, and authenticity. Through riding—and any activity we enjoy with them—they teach us much about confidence, trust, power, love, boundaries, freedom, and how to apply it all in the many areas of our lives. No matter what horses and humans do together, a horse's true purpose for being in a human's life is to assist us in our process of personal growth and development, whether we are aware of it, willing to undertake the journey, or not.

So how can we help our horses? As discussed in Chapter Five, the important first step is taking responsibility for our own health—physically, emotionally, mentally, and spiritually. In this way, they are less likely to take on our energies to the degree that they become ill or stressed. This doesn't mean that we should blame or berate ourselves if our horses get sick. There are many

other reasons animals become ill. As they evolve, all animals become more compassionate, and are more able to naturally release
these energies. But for us, the key is self-responsibility, finding
out what we can do on our end to help them. We need to become
aware of what needs healing in ourselves and in our lives, and
then begin the process.

There are other forms of responsibility we have in improving and maintaining the health of our horses as well. One of the
first things to do is to make sure you have the right horse for
you. Some humans think they can find any horse they like and
make him become the horse they want him to be. This is not
the case. Horses have individual personalities, needs, passions,
and soul purposes. Because horses live outdoors, and movement
and activity promote their health and well-being, it is important
that we share common desires and interests. If we want to be in
competition, and we pick a horse that would rather do trails or
work with kids, this could be a problem. A horse that doesn't like
competition but is forced to perform can become very depressed
or ill, and is more susceptible to injury.

Although horses always come into our lives for a reason,
sometimes the lesson is about developing the wisdom to know
what both you and your horse want, and following through with
it, even if it is necessary to let go of the horse. Obviously, it would
be helpful to have this information at the time of purchase, before the bond begins, avoiding any pain that comes with loss.
But this is not always possible. Sometimes we don't have access
to a horse's background, history, needs, or desires. This is when
consulting an animal communicator or having animal communication skills can come in handy (see Chapter Twelve).

In some cases, even if we don't share common interests the
horse is still meant to be in our lives, for a longer or shorter period of time. What is important is that we are willing to do what
is best for our horses, as soon as we are aware of it. We can make

compromises that support our horses' as well as our own needs and desires. For example, if our horse is part of our livelihood—working on our farm, pulling carriages, or giving rides—and we know the horse prefers working with kids or having more down time in the pasture with other horses, we can make these opportunities more available when our horse is not working.

If it is best to let your horse go, the sacrifice will teach you about non-attachment and love. When we truly love someone, we give without expecting anything in return. We are willing to let go of a desire because we want that other being to be happy. You will find that as you allow the horse to go to the human and life where he is best suited, it will open you up to finding the horse that is a perfect match for you. When the right human and horse are together, tremendous happiness and potential for success in many life areas are made available for both.

When I started considering the ways humans and horses were pairing up, and how sometimes it appeared that they were mismatched, I got information from the horse spirits that I wasn't expecting. They told me that domestic horses choose the human(s) they will be with in this lifetime. Often we have karmic ties—histories of having been together in other lifetimes or dimensions—and the loving bond has already formed.

They went on to say that the horses are willing to do whatever that human is interested in, be it showing, jumping, or trails. It is not only that they are willing, but also that the horse will have more of a preference, genetic predisposition, or personality for the kind of activity their human enjoys. This preference or ability usually continues for as long as a horse is supposed to be in that human's life; in many cases, for their whole lifetime. If a horse has a preference or passion different from his human's, or if it changes, it might be because it's time for him to move on to another human.

This is not to be mistaken for a horse who becomes injured or depressed, or can't compete or work because he needs a less intense or structured work routine. It might be that one or both of you need a break or lifestyle change. The same is true for a horse who is getting older and can no longer ride or work like he used to. It is essential that he find a human who can accept him for what he can do, so he doesn't continue to get passed on from human to human, like Angel, the horse I wrote about in Chapter Three.

We should take the time to find a place to live that will accommodate the living space and individual needs of our horses, and not give up or give them away because it's too difficult. I have found this to be the case with cats and dogs as well, where their owners give them up because they can't find a place that allows pets or has a yard or outdoor space that a specific animal desires or needs. I've met too many animals who feel heartbroken and abandoned in these situations, later developing behavior problems or disease. Keep looking. If you really want your animal to be in your life, and you are flexible and persistent, by the power of the law of attraction you will find the right place (or it will find you).

It is best if we can commit to having our animals in our lives for their whole lifetime at the time we buy or adopt them, but sometimes our lives change in ways we can't predict. In worst-case scenarios, you might have to place your animal in a temporary home, at a friend's or foster family's, while you tend to your own personal needs, endeavors, or financial stability. But before you leave them, I recommend you tell them what is happening and when you plan on returning to them, if you know you will. See Chapter Twelve for instructions on how to communicate with your animals.

When you have made your decision, and found the horse that is aligned with your lifestyle and hobbies, all will feel at ease.

That is not to say that problems or concerns won't arise or you won't be aware that there are things to work on. But you will experience a great comfort with your horse, a sense that all is well. There will also be fervent emotions experienced between the two of you—love, joy, bliss—leading to a delightful friendship based on connection and support. As Adele and Marlena McCormick shared in *Horse Sense and the Human Heart*, this bond has the potential to continue well beyond this lifetime into future incarnations. Many of us have experienced this firsthand, when after the death of our best animal friends we recognize their soul in a different animal who enters our lives. But most of all, when the right human and horse are together, both species will accept and work with each other's strengths and limitations. They care so deeply for the other's well-being, that both horse and human make an effort to assist in the other's happiness and fulfillment.

While I was starting to attract in more clients who wanted animal communication and healing sessions, not just with horses, but also with cats, dogs, and other animals, I began to receive more information from the horse spirits. They directed me to get my own website, teach workshops, and give lectures about what horses wanted in their relationships with humans. And so I did. As I led these talks, I could always feel the collective horse consciousness connect with me, weaving in me a desire for justice, a determination to bring about change. They really wanted things to be different between humans and horses. They wanted us to finally understand!

The qualities of change needed in horse/human relationships were respect, cooperation, dignity, and equality. Horses have historically been our greatest, most loyal servants in war, transportation, and agriculture, and now are companions and sport-mates (if we compete). They consider us partners, but are tired of the domination that has occurred over the centuries, and continues still today. As partners, they would like us to treat them as we would our most beloved family and friends.

ENDING ALL ABUSE

I am not in favor of using force or domination, including hitting our horses, with or without an object. In Chapters One and Three I discussed this, as well as the many ways horses have lived as beasts of burden, subjected to whips, spurs, heavy bits and saddles, rein yanking, and being forced to pull heavy carts and equipment. I realize we are talking about enormous animals here, but these are also very sensitive animals.

Based on my experiences as an animal communicator and rider, and having used my fair share of heavier bits, saddles, and spurs, I would not encourage you to ride bareback, with bitless bridles, or even lightweight bits if your riding experience and the horse's level of training will not permit it safely. If you use heavy gear or your horse performs laborious tasks, make sure the gear fits him appropriately, and he gets ample rest and replenishment after activities.

I recommend that you avoid even the light use of crops and spurs, because they are too easy to use in a physically abusive manner. Instead, develop ground work skills and learn energy-based training methods that promote a willing partnership. When your ground work and riding skills have advanced, if you continue to improve your communication and connection with your horse, you will eventually eliminate your need to use heavier gear and tools for pleasure and competitive riding.

Abuse can also be mental and/or emotional, or involve neglect. If we yell at our horse in frustration because he won't do what we want, if we use profanity with anger, calling him "stupid" or worse, the horse will pick up on the aggressive energy behind our language, whether he actually understands the words or not (and I have found many animals do understand words). This can cause confusion and emotional pain in the horse, much like it does in a human. At first, it might appear as though you have established leadership, as your horse scrambles to obey your commands or quickly stops doing something you tell him not to do.

But since his actions are fear-based reactions, the wanted behavior will not always be consistent. Learning can only take place when the horse feels safe and is calm to slightly aroused, not when he's in survival mode. If the mental/emotional abuse becomes frequent, a horse might eventually associate his fear with you, and this will show up more and more in your interactions. In many cases, the horse may act out by bolting off, rearing up, or kicking and bucking.

Only trust can lead to consistent and reliable outcomes and a healthy horse that doesn't eventually become distressed or despondent. The way to develop trust with your horse involves starting off with respect. They are a sentient being, just like you, with preferences, physical needs, a certain level of intelligence (which I find high among most horses), thoughts, and emotions. They therefore deserve the same kindness and consideration that you would want for yourself. Equality and dignity go hand-in-hand with respect. To me, this is about putting ourselves in our horse's hooves. Imagine for a moment what it would be like to be a horse—actually living in that physical form, experiencing your life through their senses. What would you want? How would you like to be treated?

I believe all animals have highly developed thought patterns and emotional states, even if their brains are different than ours. I have felt them experience everything from the basic feelings of peace, joy, fear, and sadness, to the more complex emotions of jealousy, animosity, amusement, embarrassment/shame, and loneliness. As Temple Grandin shared in her book *Animals in Translation: Using the Mysteries of Autism to Decode Animal Behavior,* "Animals are visual creatures," they think in pictures.[1] Volumes of information, including emotions, thoughts, words, and physical sensations can be expressed through one single message or image. This is how animals communicate with each other and with us.

On top of this, because of their energetic intimacy with their humans, their heightened sensitivity and clairvoyant natures, all animals have a tendency for precognition, the ability to see into the future. In some cases, they know what's going to happen simply because they've picked up on your thoughts or plans. I have communicated with many animals who told me (and were often worried or excited about) things that were coming up for their humans—moves, new relationships, jobs, career changes, and health issues.

When I asked the humans about it, they were often able to validate the information I received. In certain circumstances, the humans weren't able to confirm decisions or changes they hadn't yet made or experienced, but I often found out later that the animals' insights proved to be true. Because animals are a different species, with a different brain and level of cognition, as Grandin shared in *Animals in Translation,* they are even more worthy of being honored and understood by us, so they can live easier, more enjoyable lives.

GREY AND T.J.
Dignity and Cooperation

I had a session with a horse client that exemplified how much dignity and equality his human wanted him to experience. His name was Grey. Grey was a short-statured, gray Lipizzan horse that retired from ranching. He also worked at a carnival held several times a year, giving carriage rides, and he gave street carriage rides on the weekends as well. After his retirement, he was sold and taken to the property of John, his new owner. John wanted me to ask Grey what he wanted to do for the rest of his life. John loved horses, and was open to doing just about anything with them.

He ran a community program for adults with mental and physical disabilities. His program allowed them to interact with the ten to twelve horses in the herd through activities such as riding, grooming, haltering, feeding, and sometimes just observing them in pasture. John expressed that he worried about the riding. Because he lived a hardworking life, pulling carriages and giving rides, John specifically wanted to know if letting his clients ride Grey would hurt his dignity or pride. John sensed that this activity somehow caused him to feel awkward or humiliated.

When I checked in with Grey, I immediately knew what John meant. Grey's energy reflected a very masculine, stoic, majestic soul. When I asked him what he wanted to do, he looked back at me with confusion in his eyes. He seemed to be asking, "What... What?" I clarified my question by asking him if he still wanted humans to ride him. I also asked if there was anything specific he wanted to do with John, or if he just wanted to hang out with the herd for now.

This time he looked back at me and glared. "What do you mean not ride? I have always given rides, my whole life!" I could see the shock and horror register on his face, so I went on to explain further. I told him that John just wanted him to be happy in his retirement and that he could now do whatever he wanted. His facial expressions softened from disbelief to appreciation as the kindness that was offered to him sunk in. But as his muzzle quivered and he faced forward again, I knew he was still process-ing these unexpected questions.

He finally told me that he did not completely enjoy all the activities that went on in the program, but he liked riding with John so far. For now, he would appreciate some free time with the herd, particularly the two mares he had easily bonded with. After he finished telling me this, I again noticed him peer at me, still shocked, as if trying to figure me out. It seemed as though he was perplexed as to why any human would ask these kinds of questions. Then he finally stated the obvious. "No one has ever asked me this before. No one has ever asked me what I wanted. It has always been about what they have wanted."

With that, a big tear appeared in the corner of his left eye. Since horses cannot physically weep and Grey was normal-ly emotionally reserved, I knew this was of huge significance. Having kept my distance from him out of respect up until this point, I asked if I could approach. When I got the affirmative, I stood next to Grey, showing my support and compassion. I felt love swell inside, responding to his humility and gratitude, and I too had tears in my eyes.

The whole experience was one I will never forget, as I ponder the hard work and dedication that horses lend to our lives, rarely getting to live a life that they choose, many times spending their time entertaining us—being on display for our pleasure, whether at the circus or in the stables.

While I'm on the topic of dignity, I can't help but relay the story of a short exchange I once had with a horse that had a lasting effect on me, giving me a feeling of sacred reverence for these magnificent beings. I had attended a shamanic event that included riding horses to reach higher levels of spiritual awaken-ing. On my way out of the ranch, I was drawn to what appeared to be a white and gray horse standing next to the barn.

It was dark out, and his coat was a silvery sheen in the moonlight. When I stopped in front of him, I noticed he picked up on my energy right away and seemed to recognize who I was and what I was up to. He bowed in front of me, in the only way you could imagine a horse bowing. He literally bent his knees and tipped his head before me.

Like beholding a noble king, I was awed and enchanted by what I can only describe as the highest level of honor, respect, and admiration, yet so much humility, coming from another being. Radiating the same emotions I naturally felt in his presence, for him and his species, I bowed back in return. He told me he was thankful for all I was doing to help horses, and for helping humans understand them better. I told him that I was grateful for all that he was doing to help humans. I knew that he was one of the horses involved in helping to expand the consciousness of the humans that night, and I sensed he was highly evolved and had great healing power.

Although our interaction was cut short by the interruption of the people leaving the event, it altered the course of my life, reaffirming my mission to help this often misunderstood species, and giving me the determination and perseverance to see it through. In this mystical exchange, it felt as though the silver horse and I were ambassadors for our individual species, sharing information and appreciation for each other. It was as if our contact somehow bridged the gap between the human and animal worlds, making it easier for both sides to communicate, connect, and understand that each species is more similar to the other than we might normally think.

As I reflect on the experience now, it still warms my heart. The amount of love flowing between us in that moment where time and space didn't exist was something comparable to being transported back to Source, what many call God—the place of our soul's origin. In that pristine moment, I felt completely fulfilled, tranquil, and one with the universe. Ever since, I've wanted to bring that love, as well as the respect, dignity, honor, admiration, and humility back to the human culture, so we can change how we view and relate to horses, our equal partners, brothers and sisters in this physical world.

When we begin to treat our horses equally, with dignity, honor, and respect, they will naturally be more cooperative with us. By cooperation, I mean that both horse and human consider each other's opinions, ideas, and desires. We work together for each other's benefit.

A friend of mine introduced me to a horsewoman who invited me to stay on her ranch in Northern California while I was visiting the area for a few weeks. While I was there, Jane, the ranch owner, told me she was having trouble getting her horse to cooperate with her. Many times while riding, T.J., a white Peruvian Paso with a black mane, would stop abruptly. It was either difficult or impossible to get her going again. Jane was unsure how this habit got started. T.J. was well trained, formerly owned for ten years by an experienced cattle rancher who rode her every day.

She was perfectly accommodating when she was taken out with the other horses. It was only when she was ridden alone that she would decide the ride was over, usually when she was close enough to the barn to hear the other horses calling her. I told Jane that this was a common, challenging issue with riding. Because of their prey nature, horses are biologically driven to stay close to their herd. They are safer in numbers than on their own, so many horses won't feel comfortable venturing out alone.

Jane explained to me that this had occurred off and on for as long as she owned T.J., but it had become worse over the last two to three years, after her mother passed away. She spent three months in deep grief, with not even the faintest desire to go for a ride. She was also afraid that her grief would somehow negatively influence T.J.'s well-being, or make her feel even more uncomfortable with riding. During the time she was grieving and not riding, Jane made sure to turn out T.J. at least twice a day with the other horses in a nearby pasture. She thought T.J. got enough exercise there, and the horse seemed calm and content when she would go out daily to feed and talk with her.

Since I was staying at her ranch, Jane offered to let me ride T.J. I found out T.J. wasn't doing as well as Jane had thought. She was overweight, finicky, and barn sour. After about ten to fifteen minutes of what appeared to be her intolerance of riding, which included very slow walking and a few skips here and there, even with a great amount of leg squeeze, energetic and verbal encouragement on my part, T.J. would simply refuse to move forward. In her stubborn, immobile, leg-locked stance, she would look back at the other horses in the barn, as if she was missing out on something. No matter how much I tried to urge her forward using my heels and the reins, she would simply turn her body to one side and move around in a circle, instead of going ahead. Her body felt tense underneath me, as she clearly struggled against my requests.

So I decided it was best to connect with T.J. on the ground, in a more non-threatening position. I had already discovered that meeting horses on an equal level could help you re-establish a bond and leadership, leading to better results while riding. Especially when it comes to barn sour horses, any kind of pleasurable, bonding activity will inspire them to want to spend more time with you and be motivated to follow your direction.

Practicing basic horsemanship skills on the ground is an important way to help you figure out what is going on with any horse, partly because you and the horse are in a less vulnerable position than during riding, so any fear is decreased or eliminated. You can also view the horse more easily and completely, especially when checking for lameness. Best of all, ground activities are a way to figure out whether a problem you have only occurs when you ride the horse, which can help you narrow down the potential causes and more easily find a solution.

I spent time grooming and leading T.J. in a large arena. Because she now seemed more content, and didn't object to walking with me, I took her off the lead line and asked her to move forward at a pace of her own choosing, using my energy and voice. She moved forward consistently and without hesitation while in the arena. I was also aware that the horse barn was close by and well within earshot, although T.J. didn't appear distracted.

Since I had her attention, I took some time to talk to her on a deeper level. I asked her if she liked riding and wanted to continue. I told her that Jane wanted to ride for fun and companionship, and that it wasn't about performance or work. I further expressed to T.J. and Jane that riding would assist Jane in her healing process and would also keep both of them physically active. Now that Jane was grounded, beyond the initial overwhelm that comes with the beginning stages of grief, and actively processing her emotions, it was unlikely that she'd trigger an empathic reaction in T.J., such as bolting off or bucking.

It was clear that T.J. loved Jane dearly, as she affectionately groomed Jane and nuzzled her neck. It didn't seem as though she disliked riding or was in any pain. There was just a feeling of boredom and disinterest. It reminded me of a teenager who doesn't want to go to school, and announces to their mom that they are staying home. Of course if they knew they were going to learn something interesting that day, perhaps participating in their favorite activity or having a visit from a special guest, maybe they would change their mind. Although I had only planned to go for a ride that day, I wanted to give back to Jane for letting me stay with her. I wanted to uncover some information that might help reignite T.J.'s desire for riding.

At first she showed me a flash of the man who owned her last—the cattle rancher. Jane described him as "a very good horseman who was kind to the horses." I saw this as T.J. showed me a picture of a ride with the rancher. I watched as T.J. followed all his commands, moving forward, and appearing to enjoy herself. She seemed to be present in her body, and I was glad for that. She was bright-eyed and interactive with the other horses who skipped along beside her. I noticed she flattened her ears and tried to move ahead of the lead horse as the ride continued. She seemed to feel frisky, light-hearted, and free.

Then she showed me a picture of herself, alone in a pasture. There were no other horses around. The pasture was enclosed by a wrought-iron fence. She paced back and forth for what seemed like hours as I watched the sun change positions in the sky. She was clearly very anxious and worried. I asked Jane about it and she told me it must have been something that occurred on the property of a previous owner. The pasture for her horses was not contained by such a fence. I knew this was somehow connected to T.J.'s unwillingness to ride consistently without other horses, but I didn't yet have all the pieces of the puzzle.

As I walked away to get more ground work toys, I got another flash of insight. The cattle rancher rode her alone to the place of the wrought-iron fence and then left her there. I don't know how long she spent at that place, but I began to understand that she was associating riding alone with being left behind. Jane told me that the cattle rancher had taken T.J. on plenty of rides with the other horses at the ranch. She must have felt safer riding with other horses, knowing she wouldn't be left alone.

With this information I relayed to T.J. that she would never be left alone in a pasture again, and that when Jane took her out riding alone, she was doing it so they could spend time together, have fun, and be healthy. I provided some energy healing, helping her to release the trauma and residual emotions related to feeling alone and abandoned.

I recommended to Jane that she engage in daily horsemanship skills on the ground with T.J., which would help build a relationship with her in a way that would not involve riding. These exercises could include grooming, leading T.J. in the arena and other places away from the barn, and walking with her, at liberty. This would also help T.J. get used to doing other activities without the horses, gradually working up to riding again.

Over the next few weeks, Jane told me that she was successful walking T.J. on the trails, where she seemed to enjoy the activity and hadn't refused to move forward. On top of this, Jane and her friend had each ridden T.J. on the trails once without any other horses, and T.J. again had cooperated from start to finish. As I stood by listening to Jane tell me this, T.J. made eye contact with me, and licked and chewed. In that moment, I knew that she understood everything I had told her the few weeks before.

Several months later, Jane reported to me that she had discovered the farther she took T.J. from the barn, the more often she completed a ride. Previously, due to her busy lifestyle, Jane had frequently ridden her around the pasture and barn area only. She found out that T.J. didn't appear as excited about doing anything but eating and socializing with her friends when she was that close to them.

T.J. was also more reluctant to be taken out for rides during feeding time, so Jane changed the order of things. Instead of feeding and then riding her, she did it in the reverse. They now spent most of their time together on the trails, where T.J. often got her mind off the other horses and became interested in galloping and exploring the wildlife. Not only was T.J. cooperating with Jane, but Jane had cooperated with T.J. by taking the time to understand what was bothering her and how to make things easier. T.J. now had every reason to enjoy riding with Jane alone. And she still had plenty of time spent with her favorite horse friends.

CHAPTER TEN

THE BENEFITS OF A NATURAL LIFESTYLE

Another year later, and things were moving forward in my life. I began working part-time at a horse ranch. I was even more excited about the opportunity when I learned that the head rancher, Gary, was open to alternative medicine and natural ways of living for the animals. Gary owned fifteen horses. He trained, bred, and sold many, and allowed others to retire on the land in their old age. He wanted his horses to live the healthiest, most comfortable lifestyle.

From the beginning, I loved the work. I felt like I was finally home, in a place I belonged and in a world I understood. Not only did I feel balanced on a body-mind-spirit level working with nature in this way, but it also seemed like this was another reason I had the gifts that I did—like I was born to do this work!

Within the first month there, I was introduced to Dan, one of the ranch hands. His role was to provide horse caretaking duties—feeding, grooming, mucking stalls, medicating, and giving them exercise. The moment I met him, I became aware that there was more than one connection between us. We both grew up in the Midwest, and he was related to a family friend. But I also had one of those old, familiar feelings, as if we had already spent a lifetime together. I remember the first conversation we had, when we talked about the animals. He was one of the few ranch hands I had known who did not use force when working with horses, not for any reason.

I told him how I wanted to reach horse people, helping them to know and understand their horses better. I shared that I thought horses often felt confused, hurt, or betrayed by humans, when they had owners or trainers who were dominant and abusive in their behaviors. We laughed together as we discussed some of the old, outdated belief systems that many horse people have continued to carry that are obviously not true, like the idea that horses are stupid.

As I was quickly discovering in the animal communication world, all animals are aware of a whole lot more than we thought they were, including many of the private aspects of our lives. How was it, after how far horses and humans have come on this journey of evolution together, that we still didn't get them? When would our true partnership begin?

It wasn't long—maybe within our first two conversations, before I started to feel attracted to and affectionate towards Dan. The exciting feelings of passion and joy danced through me as I knew this was already love. I could sense he felt the same. When we talked he seemed shy, looking down and speaking softer, hiding behind his curly brown, shoulder-length hair. I guess it was love at first sight, or maybe it was the love that we shared in other lifetimes that made it so obvious to me. In either case, I had never felt anything this powerful with another human in my life.

But intuitively, I knew I had to wait for him to make the first move. I wanted to run to him, but he had to be ready and able, or his fear from my approach would cause him to bolt like a spooked horse. Being a direct and forthright person, the waiting was the hardest thing for me to do.

In the meantime, I had a chance to learn more about horses who were raised very differently than the ones I had met so far. These horses had about a hundred acres to graze on, and they spent most of their days out in pasture with the herd. In many ways, they lived like wild horses, although Gary did provide extra food and shelter when needed. In California, with such dry or dead vegetation most of the year, horses aren't easily able to live naturally. If they were wild, they would need to continuously move on to another location where there is a fresh, abundant supply of vegetation to graze on.

I also got to know the deeper, spiritual side of horses at this ranch. I saw how whole and sound they were, their spirits fully intact from living in such a natural way. They were not forced to do things they wouldn't instinctually want to do, and they were not squeezed into small and contained quarters. I saw this from an even more expanded viewpoint than in the case of a horse like Martie, whose story I discussed in Chapter Four. She was healed through living off the land, connecting to Earth, and deciding on her own time when she was ready to interact with the herd and humans.

These horses simply reflected freedom to me. They didn't have the emotionally tense and exhausted or underactive appearance that I saw in many domestic horses. They also seemed open to humans, yet at the same time, not preoccupied by a human's presence, as if they must fulfill some need, be wary of something or someone, or beg for attention or food.

HARRIET AND BROWNIE
Taken From the Wild

I met and worked with a horse named Harriet who taught me the profundity of horses' spiritual and biological needs. She was a pure black Mustang, with a star on her forehead. She had a small filly, named Brownie after her chocolate color, who was always attached to her side. Dan told me that Harriet had been rescued after a roundup.

A roundup is when a group of wild horses are herded up and taken out of their natural habitat in certain areas of the U.S. According to the Animal Rescue Unit (ARU), "The reasons the Bureau of Land Management (BLM) gives for the mass round-ups, is that the wild horses are starving and causing deterioration to the land."[1] But the ARU also shared that there is conflicting data revealing that the land the horses are taken off of is being used for cattle grazing and mining projects. After the horses are rounded up, it is then required that they are advertised for adoption, but as told in the documentary *Wild Horses and Renegades: A Modern Day Western*, many horses that are not adopted are often shipped out of the country for slaughter. [2]

Sadly, this is an all-too-common occurrence in the U.S. The horses are kept temporarily in holding pens until a home can be found for them. As shown in the documentary and frequently reported by various animal rights groups on social media websites, many of the horses rounded up are injured or die en route to these holding pens. They succumb to the stress, dehydration, starvation, and exhaustion that happens when they run for many miles in the rounding up process, being chased by helicopters or trucks. After being placed in the holding pens, many more horses become ill or die because of improper living conditions, including inadequate food and water consumption.

The rescue where Harriet ended up quickly became full. This is a common situation in the current economic decline, with many people losing their jobs and being unable financially to continue to care for their horses. People are even leaving their horses attached to the bumpers of cars or to fences outside of rescues, with the hope that the rescue can take them in and find them a new home. In addition, horses cost more than they have in the past, with the price of hay going through the roof. The fees at most boarding facilities are rising so they can afford to pay for food and resources needed to house and care for the horses, which perpetuates this vicious cycle. Fortunately, the owner of the rescue Harriet was sent to knew Gary, and asked if he had room for her. Gary agreed to take her.

Dan asked me if I could look into what was going on with Harriet and Brownie. Harriet recently developed an acute upper respiratory infection (URI) and diarrhea. Dan was doing everything he could to support her immune system, including giving her antibiotics, supplements, anti-inflammatories, and rest. Now Brownie was starting to show signs of the illness.

I decided to talk with Brownie first, thinking she would be the easiest to interact with. Through her short life experience, she was sure to be the more innocent, less jaded. But as soon as I began interacting with her, mother Harriet stepped in. I started to explain to her that my intent was to just help Brownie feel better, when she interrupted, "I know, I know. Listen, I have something to share here."

I nodded my head to let her know I was listening.

"This is an outrage. This is unbelievable. Do you have any idea what happened to us? They took me away from my family. It's only my baby and myself here, that's it. I miss my partner and the others in the herd. Where are they? Do you know where I can find them? Can you bring me back to them?"

Astonished by the anguish of this beautiful, powerful mare, I sat for a moment, unable to speak. She sent me images of herself and her herd or band—a breathtaking array of multi-colored and spotted Mustangs, Paints, and Appaloosas. I saw much focused, possessive, stud-like behavior, so I knew there were stallions; but many mares, fillies, and colts of various ages also accompanied them. This was her family.

One picture kept showing up over and over in my mind. I saw a large, muscular Paint stallion. I knew the horse was male and I knew it was her partner, although I can't explain how. Seen through my inner vision, the intensity of their connection was impeccable. I knew what that was all about. It was a feeling that could not be mistaken. Only two lovers could radiate the passionate bond I was feeling through my physically painful heart. I watched as the stallion looked at her in my mind with eyes like deep liquid wells, mixed with love, sorrow, and remorse.

As I processed the enormity of the impact and consequences of these images, emotions, and physical sensations, I was reminded of the extent of a horse's need and desire to be in contact and connection with their own loved ones, like the stories of Martie and Blue from Chapter Four. Unlike us, horses like Harriet that grow up wild are much like natives who are born in tight-knit communities that actively care for each member as if they were family. I knew intuitively that, especially for horses, more than any other species, this is an emotional and spiritual need that must be fulfilled to maintain health. It is the basis for why it is recommended that you always have more than one horse, or at least keep your horse boarded or in pasture with other horses.

I knew there was not much I could do to help Harriet. She would likely be at this horse ranch for the rest of her life. I explained to her the dilemma. To the best of my ability in horse language, I told her that I was sorry there were humans doing things with and to horses that bring great sadness and disharmony. I perceive this tragedy as a human disease, a fault or weakness on our part. Unfortunately, her herd was in another state. I did not even know if they were still there or alive. She would have to get used to this place as her home. She would have to grieve the loss of her loved ones.

She appeared to be processing what I had told her as she paced back and forth in the stall she was temporarily kept in (when Dan gave her medications). When she came back to me at the fence she told me she understood what I had told her, although the anger and grief over what was done were like heavy weights sagging her physical posture and energy field. I could also sense a lingering fear in her, related to being pushed out of her natural habitat so violently and quickly in the roundup.

I decided to do some healing work with her. But before I even got started with Harriet, I was amazed to see her Divine Self's clear and strong connection with her physical self and her personality. Even though she had been taken from her family and off the land she lived on, she still maintained the alignment to the sacred place inside that is true. Her will had not been broken, and she didn't strike me as one who would normally be easily intimidated or manipulated by human behavior. I associated this with her strong start in life—living among her herd and with the natural cycles of Mother Nature.

Because of this, when I did the healing with Harriet she was able to make the quickest, easiest, most graceful shift. I worked with the appropriate sacred geometric shapes within the universal energy field (see Chapter Twelve for more information on sacred geometry) to help her release the anger and fear that she experienced during the roundup. I channeled healing energy from the horse spirits to help her transmute the grief into self-love.

Immediately, I noticed a change in her energy field. It was lighter and more radiant. I continued to stay with her for another fifteen to twenty minutes integrating light and color with her energy fields to help her assimilate the healing, as well as helping her physical body release any disease created because of the anguish. When I finished, she whispered her thanks to me, and then hurried off to the back of her stall to attend to her filly.

The following week I came back to check on both of them. Dan told me Harriet and Brownie had already made progress. The fast respiratory rate and fever associated with the URI were gone, and so was the diarrhea. Brownie's beginning symptoms had disappeared as well. I was delighted to hear how quickly they had begun the healing process.

Over the course of the next few weeks, Harriet and Brownie continued to improve in health and well-being. I did a couple more healing sessions with both of them. With Harriet, I focused on helping her clear any remaining pent-up emotions related to the roundup, which would also open her up to the spiritual mastery attained through this release. These emotions had caused her physical body to go into stress mode, which led to the URI and diarrhea. When all the toxic energy related to the emotional negativity was released, her health easily went back into balance.

As for Brownie, I saw that she was influenced by her mother's illness and strife. She picked up on her emotional patterns, which led to the same physical problems. This happened even though she was born at the ranch, never experiencing the traumatic roundup. Therefore, when Harriet healed, so did she. I did very little individual healing with Brownie. This just goes to show how easy it is to take on the vibrations of those close to us without consciously knowing or meaning to!

On the rare occasions I've been able to work with wild horses and animals, I've discovered they don't have as much emotional baggage, or the difficulty in releasing it, as domesticated animals do. The reason many domesticated animals, like their fellow humans, are challenged in these areas is because they live with and are influenced by us. That is why they often develop human-like characteristics.

Humor me for a moment, while I give you an example to illustrate this truth. Imagine you are kidnapped by aliens at birth. How long would you need to be in their company, with all your needs met, being showered with love and attention, especially without ever having known your biological family, before you would start to become like them? Think about it. Now envision many years going by. Do you speak their language yet? What kind of behavior and emotional patterns do you think you would pick up over time?

Regardless of our influence on the domestic animals in our lives, based on my experience as an animal healer, most let go of physical, mental, and emotional pain faster than we do because they do not have the ego consciousness that we do. Our minds tend to be our biggest obstacles when it comes to healing, because we keep old references to what is familiar, what we believe to be true, and we create stories around these beliefs to keep them real in our lives. Animals don't carry these same fabricated stories and belief systems.

For this reason, animals don't develop the kinds of resentments and hatreds that cause violent tendencies in humans. As Temple Grandin shared in *Animals in Translation*, most aggression in animals is instinctually based, or due to an external trigger; for example, if you look or act in some way like a person who abused them in the past. Horses in particular are never instinctually aggressive, because they are prey animals. If they act aggressively, they have either been mistreated and are protecting themselves against further abuse or pain, or they are empathically picking up on your anger and fear and acting them out. In either case, it is our responsibility to figure out what is going on, and make the necessary changes.

If they have been mistreated, we must have patience with them while they develop trust again. An abused child that comes to live with a foster family will often misbehave because that is the only way he or she knows how to survive. Whether it is a child or horse in these circumstances, we must have compassion and develop appropriate boundaries, but never harm.

You might be wondering what to do about those horses who come to you from another human who has mistreated them, or with whom you have started off on the wrong foot, perhaps letting the horse dominate you. A true partnership exists when both horse and human work together, not where either one of you overpowers the other. This is often the bigger reason behind why a particular horse has come into our lives—to help us master a particular lesson, such as empowerment.

I recommend looking at your past patterns in relationships with humans to discern whether the horse is teaching you a lesson or if he needs healing. Does the horse fight you on every simple command? Ask yourself if you have a repeated pattern with humans of not getting your needs met or not being heard, understood, or respected. Perhaps you have a lesson to learn about self-worth or assertiveness. When you find the source of the problem, get the tools and resources needed to shift your energy into empowerment, or get the horse the healing he needs. You may discover that you *and* your horse need healing.

As well as having karmic connections with us through the deep bonds we often formed in many lifetimes together, horses can be drawn to us for other reasons that can affect their overall health and well-being. Many times there is a resonance between a horse and human, which often leads to instant attraction, especially in cases where a human feels right away that he must buy, ride, or spend time with a particular horse. As I discussed in Chapter Four, physical, mental, or emotional resonance between a human and horse increases the likelihood that both have had similar thoughts, feelings, and life experiences.

As Linda Kohanov wrote in *Riding Between the Worlds*, many abused horses will attract a human who has been abused.[3] Horses who dissociate from their bodies often have humans who dissociate. In these examples, there is a great potential for healing, as both parties will feel completely understood and comfortable with the other. The downfall is that either species can easily trigger the other into a panicked, dissociative state.

Unfortunately, while riding, this is an accident waiting to happen. In cases like this, as Kohanov discussed, it might be wise for an easily dissociated human to have a solid, steady, grounded horse or vice versa. Otherwise, it takes a great degree of awareness on the part of the human to navigate the riding with caution and ease, so that both horse and human remain physically safe and emotionally balanced.

ENDINGS AND BEGINNINGS

As time went on at the ranch, things became tense between Dan and me. To my dismay, instead of taking the initiative and asking me out, I found that Dan withdrew from me more and more with each passing day. At first there were awkward, uncomfortable moments of silence in our conversations, even when trying to discuss work-related topics. Later, it seemed that he would avoid me altogether. I would look for him on the ranch to ask him about a horse's progress or let him know about some intuitive information I had received, and he would either talk to me in a clipped, brief manner, or answer as he walked away.

The tension was culminating, and it was almost too much to bear. I could feel the conflicting emotions in him. I knew he was petrified, yet still interested. And there remained a physical attraction that was hard to ignore. I spent many nights picking up the phone and then putting it back into its receiver with defeat. I knew he wouldn't want to talk to me if he was running away from me. I felt helpless. The love of my life was right in front of me, I knew it. I could feel it in my bones. And yet, we weren't together. Not only was he scared, but he wasn't ready, and he might not even want a relationship.

By this time, I was having regular conversations with my guides and the horse spirits. In the beginning, they told me to wait, to give him time and the chance to be ready. They told me it was essential that I wait for his move and not directly approach him, that I needed to be subtle or I'd push him away. But that was already happening.

So I tried to reach him the only way I knew how. I talked to him about the horses as much as I could while we worked, to try to reignite the joy that came up in both of us when we connected through our shared livelihood and passion. I felt that my body language would let him know that I was still available and interested, as I was always open and receptive to him, always trying to make eye contact. But he eventually refused to look at me or engage with me. Now, whenever I was in his presence he pulled his energy back, avoiding the warm, nurturing exchange I knew we both relished. He was shutting me out. There was nothing else I could do but back off and give him space.

And yet I still waited. I waited for months and months. Why did I wait so long? There were so many reasons for us to be together—why I didn't want to give up: our shared passion for horses and a similar approach to working with them, the love that was already palpable between us since the day I met him, and the chemistry we shared. Not to mention, I adored his sweet, tender nature, the gentle way he handled the horses and how much he cared for them. He was a kind, good-hearted man.

On top of this, the horse spirits and my personal guides told me there was still a chance. They also told me that he was my soulmate, and that together we had the potential of doing healing work with horses and animals, benefitting their lives and their humans. We could help bridge the gap between animals and humans, improving communication and understanding, and helping all live together harmoniously. I can still remember the image they sent me, of the two of us together, with huge fireworks going off where our energy fields merged. Above us were the words *Soul's Purpose* in glittered letters. I shuddered as the visceral impact of this registered in my body. Whenever I wanted to give up, this memory came back to me.

Another piece of information that helped me wait was something they told me early on. Dan had many issues to overcome if he wanted to be with me. He would have to master lessons around his self-esteem, confidence, and self-love. Without these qualities, he could hardly work up the nerve to ask me out. It was also very difficult for a logical and rational, primarily left-brained man to consider what his life would be like with me.

I was a woman who followed the desires of my soul and listened to and trusted my intuition. I was confident and had developed a substantial amount of personal power. His life with me would operate on a whole new level of reality. Unless he was willing and able to grow in such a short period of time, he would most likely be threatened by my power. This would either deter him from wanting to have a relationship with me at all, or block the potential for a healthy relationship once it was established.

Despite the difficulty of bearing the heart-rending burden of knowing what could be with us but probably wouldn't, I received more insights from my guides that helped me cope. If Dan didn't take the major leap forward that he needed to, there was another soulmate that would come soon after. His name was Brian. They wouldn't tell me anything about Brian, except that he was someone I would love just as much.

After eight months of giving Dan time, it became hard for me to work at the ranch. We were not communicating at all anymore, and Gary was starting to ask questions. I felt that my work wasn't going as well as it had been, and the horses were suffering at the hands of both of us because of this standoff. Although there was a part of me that still didn't want to give up, the heart-break I was feeling due to the lack of a relationship with Dan kept me from continuing to work there. I had mostly made up my mind to leave, but before I could do so, there was one thing I had to do.

On the last day of work on the ranch, I knocked on his door. I was going to tell him how I felt, whether he wanted to hear it or not. I could not go on never having expressed how I felt to him, and not being able to hear him say something in return—even if it was that he didn't want to be with me. There was a part of me that wanted to know why things had changed between us since those first few months when I started at the ranch, but then I remembered that I already knew. It was his fear. I assumed he would reject me now, but at this point that made no difference to me. I was leaving today and would never see him again. I waited, and I knew he was home, but he never answered the door. I knew then it was definitely right to move on. It was time.

The next day I moved to a two-acre organic vegetable farm with horse boarding, which I had found a couple weeks before on the Internet. I rented a small cottage available on the beautiful land. I felt a sense of relief, as it was a new beginning in my life. I had no idea what was in store for me at the farm, but I did know I needed to heal from what had happened at the ranch. Even though we didn't ever have a single date, it was as if a lifetime of love had disappeared into thin air. I didn't know how I was going to get over Dan, but I would find a way.

I found comfort in a few friends who were also healing professionals that I had met while taking energy healing courses over the past year. I spent as much time as I could with the horses on the property, getting to know a few of their humans in the process. I also did a couple more healing sessions with Renée.

Several months passed, and I was beginning to feel like my old self again. By this time, my intuitive and healing career had taken a turn for the better. Although I had a loss in my personal life, I had gained a tremendous amount of professional exposure through my website, referrals, and appearances at healing expos around California. I had also branched out and was now doing intuitive and healing work with humans too.

Many of the owners of my animal clients wanted sessions for themselves. I was nervous about it at first, wondering how it would be, if doing this work with humans would go the same way it did with animals. But when I began, I discovered it worked almost exactly the same, and in fact was much easier. Because humans could talk out loud, they gave me a starting point for accessing the energy, instead of my having to rely on symbols, words, physical sensations, emotions, and pictures to begin the intuitive process.

Working with animals also taught me how to understand what was going on physically or medically with the body in both species. Because the animals couldn't verbalize what was going on with their health, and often were not directly in my presence, I would use my second sight to view the blueprint or etheric aspect of their physical body. Then I would look at which areas of the body were affected, and what was causing the physical problems their humans reported. Because of my background and education in nursing, I knew what many of these body imbalances or illnesses were.

Once with a dog client, I saw inflammation in the sac around his heart. I knew from my earlier training that this was called pericarditis, which is a very serious health condition. I told his human this, and to take him to the vet right away. The vet was able to verify that he did have pericarditis and he was treated appropriately. This was all discovered because of his human's concern that he seemed more tired lately!

As I continued to help more animals heal over the next few months, I also received healing in return from a horse I will never forget. The memory of the time in my life when I met Buster will always warm my heart. When I think back to that day, I can recall the feelings of adjusting to a new place of living, new landlords, and the excitement and anticipation of what was coming next. I was happy with the move and change of residence because I was in a new city, a city that was open to the healing arts and had an abundant number of horses. This city was Ojai, California.

Ojai is known for being a magical, mystical place, with many spiritual vortexes that can help shift the consciousness of anyone who lives or travels through. I felt this was the perfect place and time for starting over and continuing to move forward with the success of my work. I was even starting to believe that it was likely I would be able to quit my hospital job very soon. I knew that I could meet the right people who would make it possible to double my weekly clientele.

One thing was for sure, even after all that had happened with Dan, the experience taught me that anything was possible. I had come to a fork in the road of my life. If we had begun a relationship, I would be headed in another direction—where my residence, work, and romantic life would be very different than they are now. As my guides had reminded me repeatedly, easing my mind, "You will end up with the one with whom you will be the happiest, wealthiest, and healthiest." I couldn't argue with that! I knew it was time to move on and allow a new reality to manifest.

BUSTER
A Horse That Healed a Broken Heart

When I greeted Buster that first day, I knew I had met a special friend. There was a shared emotional resonance and karma that drew me to him, because I immediately felt comfortable and at ease. I felt the desire to be affectionate with him, but hesitated. Buster looked around at me with wide eyes, and would then quickly tuck his head from view when I returned his gaze.

His human was a woman named Sam, a neighbor of mine. She told me Buster had been badly abused by humans. A group of teenage boys had beaten him with fallen branches from a nearby oak tree, while his previous owner happened to come upon the scene too late. I could also see with my second sight that he had worked as a dressage horse before, and had his head tied down. The attachments and positions of the tie-downs caused him to have neck pain from time to time, and he often had difficulty accepting a bit or wearing any kind of head gear because of it.

He made repeated attempts to peer in my direction while I was talking to Sam, so I knew Buster was interested. But he kept his distance from me physically. Emotionally, I could feel the fear and mistrust that kept him from interacting more directly, even though a part of him wanted to. Sam offered to let me groom him. As I did, Buster tensed up, keeping his head turned back as he remained on guard throughout the whole groom. I noticed he was particularly touchy when it came to his chest and poll area. Sam explained that this was where he was beaten.

Sam and I agreed that I would do some healing work with Buster. I wanted to groom him more and ride him eventually, but I knew it would be too hard on him right now, with all his defenses up. I wanted him to feel comfortable in my presence. What I didn't know yet was that he was going to heal me as much as I would heal him.

I started off most days just talking to Buster outside his stall. Then I would bring forth the healing for the trauma he went through. I used energetic tools of sacred geometry, color, and light, helping him receive all spiritual lessons, and begin to build trust again. We always got to the place of his heart, and that's where I would melt.

As I brought in the energy to heal his broken heart, I would be overcome with sorrow. There were many days I just stood there and wept. The voices of the guides said it was time to let my own heart break open, so that I would be ready to love again. Like many people who have loved and lost, I had placed an energetic barrier of protection around my heart, so no one could hurt me again. But unfortunately, that barrier also prevented me from being receptive to anyone new.

After weeks of building up the strength to open my heart again, I was finally able to let go of the emotions, and not hold anything back. I felt the deep burning sensations in my heart that went along with the emotional turmoil, the tormenting loss that suffocated me. I felt like I was shipwrecked at sea, floating in no man's land. I was shattered by life's seeming insignificance, drowning in a sinking sense of emptiness.

I knew this was the bottomless pit of sorrow and grief—perhaps from all the losses, disappointments, and betrayals in love, even beyond this lifetime. I could understand why so many people struggled with grief and loss, walking that fine line of suicidal ideation that often accompanies this type of trauma. I also understood the reverse—how the pain could be so devastating, that if unable to cope, many would suppress or repress it in order to survive. But I was blessed to feel the supportive energy of my guides around me. Like the assurance of the earth under my feet, I knew I would be okay. As long as I was true to myself through experiencing my emotions, I would see myself on the other side of this.

I worked through these feelings over the course of a few more weeks, hanging out with Buster. I took Buster on walks just by halter and lead rope. He liked this relaxing, nurturing time. I knew that he had been through a grueling training while he was a dressage horse, so I thought he'd appreciate it.

During that time, Sam told me he was starting to give her trouble while riding, not wanting to cooperate on the trails, having his own ideas about how fast or slow he wanted to go, contrary to what she wanted. Despite his past, she reported that he was usually a steady, dependable horse for most people to ride. Her other horse, Dixie, was more frisky and unpredictable. If Sam went riding with a friend or her son, she often had them ride Buster for safety, while she rode Dixie. But now Buster was becoming headstrong, demanding to have his way.

I saw this as a sign that Buster was becoming more empowered. He was tired of having to please humans, and wanted a chance to do things his way. We continued to bond and spent time without an agenda. This gave him the opportunity to play with his newfound freedom. I did ride him some, but mostly at a walk in the area around his stall. He seemed to be more relaxed and had less neck discomfort when I didn't put pressure on him to do anything fast or fancy, and when using the lightest headgear.

I usually let him lead in our rides together, so he could discover what he enjoyed about this shared human-horse activity. Other days I gave direction and guidance with riding, asking him to trot out in the meadows and trails near the farm, so he could gradually get used to a more purposeful, energetic activity again. At this time, I also suggested to Sam that she play with him in this way too, implementing similar strategies to connect to him in their new partnership based on equality. Because of his healing, he was a different horse. It would take time, practice, and healthy boundary setting before they'd find the perfect balance in their relationship together, especially with riding.

After a couple more months, Buster began to show signs of improvement. He was more comfortable letting me groom him, without the tension and neck twisting. I was even able to touch his chest without him biting the air or pinning his ears back. He was beginning to trust again. I knew he enjoyed our time together. I could see it in the way his body lightened up when I visited his stall.

My heart was feeling much better too. I now had very few days of sorrow, and more days of joy and contentment because I had gained an appreciation for all of my life experiences. The heavy emotions and hardships had taught me the importance of fully loving and becoming responsible for myself, my happiness, and my life's course, and detaching from the actions and choices of others. I recognized the beauty and grace in the darkest night of my soul, because of the profundity of it. I now knew and understood my soul's destiny.

As Adele and Marlena McCormick shared in their book *Horse Sense and the Human Heart*, feeling the full spectrum of our emotions, even with life's upheavals, allows us to see the world from an expanded viewpoint and opens us up to change—both within ourselves and in our personal lives. I was grateful to be living in a beautiful place, working with animals and humans in my own way. My future felt so promising. I sensed there was so much more coming, right around the corner—that I would be happier than I ever imagined with my work and love life. I owed part of this to Buster. Through helping him, I helped myself open my heart to love again. I began to trust that the best was possible, even if disappointments could still occur.

CHAPTER ELEVEN

THE TEACHINGS OF THE NATURE SPIRITS

It was around this time that I met a man who had come to the farm as a temporary farm hand. He worked primarily in the organic vegetable garden, but also with the herbs and flowers. When I had time off from my healing work, I was drawn to exploring in the gardens. I loved having my hands in the dirt, and often found it soothing and grounding to work in the earth this way. Even though up until this point my focus had been with animals, I was beginning to understand the calm that all of nature provided, especially for someone as sensitive as I was.

The garden was a peaceful atmosphere, and I discovered that I could use my gentle and nurturing qualities to work with these types of living beings. I provided healing for the nature kingdom—trees, plants, flowers, food, and the land—in exactly the same way I did with humans and animals. We are all made up of energy and have a Divine Self, which includes the exquisite, enlightened aspect of our being.

When I do energy work with any living being, I direct the healing energy into a specific area of their energy field that needs the healing, or to their Divine Self, so they can integrate the energies in a way that is appropriate for their individual needs. When I worked in the gardens, I tuned in to the energy fields of the plants just like I did with animals, accessing information in the form of words, phrases, colors, feelings, physical sensations, or pictures, as I perceived what was going on for them.

The farm worker's name was Brian, but when I was introduced to him I didn't think it was the Brian that my guides had told me about. I had expected that the next guy would be involved with animals somehow, although I knew he'd be very interested and passionate about nature as well. This Brian was several years younger than I was, and he wasn't actively working in the farming or animal husbandry area like I expected. This temporary job was on a whim. He told me he had felt called to come to this part of California and take this job for the summer. He didn't know why.

I was also concerned about his emotional state. My intuition told me that he was depressed, but had learned to hide it well. It was likely he spent his whole life coping, and not in such a good way. He had also shared with me that he felt lost—unsure of his direction in life. This wasn't exactly what I was expecting in my next potential mate. But then I remembered Dan and his insecurity and shyness.

Like Dan, Brian had a big leap to make if we were going to be together. But he was more gregarious than Dan, and had already started his healing and spiritual growth process through psychotherapy in his teenage years. I liked him right away, and felt the same instant connection that I felt with Dan. I got that same familiar feeling, like I had known him some other time, some other place, long ago.

For a short time, I let go of knowing how it would be with us, and simply enjoyed gardening with him. He taught me a few basic principles about planting and harvesting, helped me identify plants and learn which crops liked more or less water and sun. But by the second or third time we gardened together, I knew he had me. It was unbelievable. The physical attraction was there, even though I never knew I liked red hair, beards, and a stocky build!

The chemistry between us was mutual, and beautiful, like being in the midst of a choir of angels. It quickly grew into love. Our love was a separate entity that showed up every time we were near each other. It was gentle and calming, like smooth, all-encompassing, warm bath waters. There was always great comfort and relaxation, a sweet lightness in my heart whenever we were together. We both seemed to long for each other's presence, finding ourselves drawn together like magnets, even if we were apart for only a couple days.

I couldn't tell Brian about my feelings right away, though. I knew from my experience with Dan that I would have to wait again—that he didn't recognize me as a soulmate yet. The waiting would give him the time to figure this out, letting him decide if he was interested in a romantic relationship. We spent much time on the farm together and had many conversations about spirituality that were mutually initiated and enjoyed. Because of this, I believed there was a chance for us. This wouldn't be Dan all over again. From deep inside I knew that this time things would go differently. And for the most part, they did. Over the course of one summer, Brian continued to come forward and ask me out.

But I could feel his fear. Brian wasn't ready for a relationship. And like Dan, he was freaked out by the idea of being with someone like me. I was different than the average woman—"ethereal," as he put it. He always looked at me like he was trying to break some kind of secret code. So in those first couple months, we spent time together casually, more as friends.

Brian worked a few other jobs on farms in the area. Sometimes he'd invite me along and I always enjoyed the experience. He would work with the farmers and the crops, while I checked out the animals. In these experiences, I got to understand farm animals more, and how they needed just as much help as our domestic cats, dogs, and horses.

Farm animals, also known as livestock, have much in common with wild horses. Farm animals and wild horses generally do not incarnate to help a particular human grow or evolve. They help humanity by modeling the wisdom in their cohesive, collective energy. It is becoming more common in these changing times for livestock to be considered family to those who keep them—much like our domesticated cats and dogs. In these cases, karmic contracts can be formed, and through our bonds and friendships with these animals, they teach us personal life lessons that can expand our consciousness and transform our lives.

I began to receive this information through my contact with the horse consciousness, as well as the nature spirits and devas. Similar to what Machaelle Small Wright shared in her book *Behaving As If the God in All Life Mattered*, a deva is an aspect of a specific animal or nature collective that provides the blueprint for how each individual being is structured physiologically, as well as mentally and emotionally. There is a deva that represents each animal or living being: dog, cat, pig, chicken, horse, rose, corn, potato, and even human.

As Wright stated in her book, the nature spirits are the "workers,"[1] who receive the necessary information from the devic realm to provide the balance, stability, or changes needed to keep a living being healthy, vital, and strong. On these various farms with Brian, I saw the nature spirits with my second sight—a vibrant, white energy surrounding a certain plant or animal. As I continued to tune in to them, I felt their light, joy-filled frequencies. I knew they were the reason for the uplifting and delightful feelings many experience in a garden or natural setting.

From all my formal education and spiritual growth up until this point of my life, I had always thought of the soul and the physical body as two aspects of one's being that greatly impact each other. I believed the soul was comprised of an accumulation of all other life experiences and expressions beyond this incarnation, as well as what some call the Great Spirit or God within. In this time spent working with the farm animals, learning and communicating with the nature spirits and devas, I came to the conclusion that our physical, mental, and emotional states, although definitely affected by all of the life experiences our soul has lived, are immeasurably influenced by our biology—the genetics and temperament we inherit, as well as our current life experiences. This discovery allowed me to help even more horses.

I found this out through trial and error while working with the animals on the farms Brian and I would visit. I could connect with and ask the nature spirits to restore life force energy to a part of the body that had been constricted or blocked due to stress, which would provide physical healing and relief for that animal. I could also ask the animal's deva to make available particular genes or enzymes for better physical functioning, which could diminish or eliminate the symptoms associated with inherited diseases or syndromes.

Of course, this did not happen in every case. While practicing with farm animals, I discovered that the amount of healing that occurred was often dependent upon whether specific life lessons were mastered by the animals or humans around them. I also learned that, in some cases, with animals and humans, disease is not always experienced to learn a lesson, but can be a soul's desire to live with illness or physical limitation so that he or she can take up a certain role in life, help others, or experience a completely different way of being.

As I applied this knowledge in my healing practice with horses, I began trusting what my claircognizance, or inner knowing, had been hinting at since I began. I concluded that horses, like humans, have their own personal lessons to learn during a physical incarnation, and often spend lifetime after lifetime in the process of gaining spiritual mastery. Horses also accumulate emotional ties and baggage in their current lives and in lifetimes where they had previously known a particular human or another animal.

Through much experience gained in the many intuitive sessions I've had with horses since I started working with the farm animals, I have discovered that the soul of a horse chooses his physical form for different reasons. Some choose to live as a wild horse, experiencing all the lessons that relate to being in a horse's profoundly sensitive, sensual body, being united in a herd community, but living out the survival mechanisms that are needed when hunted in the wild. These souls help humanity adjunctively with nature as they model their comfort and ease with their physicality, and the trust, cooperation, and loyalty that comes from operating as a herd.

Other souls have lived many horse lives, while some choose a horse incarnation after living as human, other animals, or another species. I've met a few souls who had reached high levels of enlightenment and came to Earth in animal form, as a domestic horse, so they could be spiritual teachers. In their disguised horse form, they could avoid setting off human triggers such as the fear of being overpowered, controlled, or brainwashed. These are what I call guru triggers, whereby people will block healing from a human teacher because of their fear of losing their power. Horses don't set off these guru triggers. They go directly to the heart of the matter—helping us feel and release emotional hurts, resentments, betrayals, and even hatred, thereby leading us to develop compassion and unconditional love for ourselves and others.

HEALTH TIPS FROM NATURE
The Slaughter Dilemma

On a more dismal note, working with farm animals shifted my attention to the issue of animal slaughter. Like farm animals, horses are also killed for food. According to the Animal Rescue Unit (ARU), many American wild horses rounded up on U.S. lands eventually end up in slaughterhouses. After they are rounded up, the horses are kept in long-term holding pens for months or years, often unable to be placed in a permanent home. As the ARU said, "Because of the 'Burns' rider adopted into the 1971 Wild Horse and Burro Protection Act, the Bureau of Land Management, or BLM, can now sell wild horses for 10 dollars a piece [sic] to anyone, without restrictions, provided the horse has been advertised for adoption 3 times, or they are over the age of 10. ... Most kill buyers are looking for large amounts of untrained, unwanted wild horses for $10 each."[2] This is the fate of many of these horses who are then packed up and often shipped out of the U.S., to the place of their death.

At the time this book went to press, I became aware that it is also legal to slaughter horses in the U.S. again. This issue remains a complicated and contended one, and bans and amendments are in the process of being reconsidered and reintroduced, including the American Horse Slaughter Prevention Act. For more information and updates on the laws and regulations regarding commercial horse slaughter, visit the Animal Law Coalition's website at www.animallawcoalition.com. [3]

Currently, we live in a reality where controversial cultural, social, lifestyle, and health factors influence a human's decision to eat meat for nourishment. I have been both a meat-eater and a vegetarian at different times in my life because of a few of these same reasons. In some countries, it is commonplace to eat the meat of animals that are considered pets or family members in the U.S. This is an abomination to many Americans and the citizens of other countries, yet it is perfectly normal and accepted by us to consume the meat of cows, chickens, pigs, turkeys, and many types of fish.

The horse spirits have told me that there will come a day in the future when this will change. At this time, they stress the importance of our learning how to provide for and interact with the animal and nature kingdoms in a way that supports their health and well-being throughout their lifetime. For this reason, I recommend that all animal lovers, ranchers, and farmers talk to the nature spirits and devas of their animals and crops to receive instruction on how to properly care for them. In Chapter Twelve, I describe how to communicate with these aspects of your animal, which will also help you deepen your connection to them and improve their health.

There are a few health guidelines and tips that the horse deva and nature spirits would like humans to be aware of. First of all, every animal and aspect of nature needs sufficient space to grow and move about. The larger the animal or plant, the more space required. Horses in particular would prefer pastures, rather than small paddocks or stalls. If you cannot accommodate pasture living, get your horses turned out at least once a day for a few hours.

Animals and nature also appreciate a clean, quiet, non-toxic living environment. This is true not only on a physical level, but also mentally, emotionally, and energetically. Loud noises, and the disturbing thoughts and emotions associated with any potential for harm can cause physical and emotional distress in animals and nature. This idea is validated in the book *The Secret Life of Plants* by Peter Tompkins and Christopher Bird. They described how polygraph devices noted what would be considered traumatic or peaceful responses in plants that were affected by the same type of mental or emotional stimulus in a caretaking human. There is also increasing evidence available in today's world of research about the health dangers and risks in the use of chemical fertilizers, pesticides, and herbicides on our plants and animals—both to their detriment and ours.

Lastly, the animal kingdom prefers that their bodies maintain their natural integrity; that we don't alter or mutilate their physical vessel from the shape and form they were born in. For the most part, I don't think this applies to neutering or spaying animals to prevent overpopulation, especially if it's done under anesthesia. However, if there are other birth control methods available, there might be circumstances when you'd want to consider them.

In learning what I have from working with farm animals, I would never assume anything before checking with each individual animal first. They have their own preferences and opinions. Most importantly, you will find that if you honor the needs and comfort of the nature and animals you keep, not only will they be healthier, but your ranch, farm, food, and life will benefit as well.

Helping nature and animals thrive while living, and instituting compassionate processes of killing, also makes it more likely that we will consume wholesome, healthy, and nourishing foods. A chicken who lives as natural, free, and happy as possible—up to and through death—will be filled with higher vibrational energies in the body, which we consume when we eat the meat. I think we all know the lower vibrational energies; fear, anger, and sorrow are the main ones. In addition, stress hormones like adrenaline and cortisol are released when the animals feel profound rage, grief, or terror related to unfortunate living conditions and life circumstances. When we consume meat that carries these energies and hormones, it can negatively impact our physical, mental, emotional, and spiritual health. Evita Ochel, B.Sc., B. Ed., CHN, explored this idea in her online article *15 Reasons Why You May Want to Reconsider Eating Meat.*[4]

This leads us to the question of slaughtering. Different types of animals, such as horses, are killed for food in various areas of the world due to human preference and tradition. Whether we think it's right or not, animals are sacrificed to provide nourishment to many. At this time, in our gratitude for their offering to us, we can at least be as compassionate as possible in the process of taking their lives.

In her book *Animals in Translation* and as portrayed in the HBO film that bears her name, Temple Grandin, a pioneer in this field, discussed how her own experience with autism helped her understand how animals think, act, and feel. One of the things she worked passionately towards was giving cattle the most physically comfortable and fearless deaths. She created an updated slaughterhouse design; one with solid floorboards made with built-in tread, so the cattle wouldn't slip and fall, or become trapped in the cracks of the floorboards. Her new plan also consisted of solid walls to block any light that might distract the cattle, as well as a conveyer belt system that intersected with the floor. The conveyer belt was built to take them up to the place of slaughter in a manner that was gentle on their bodies, which helped them relax along the way. Grandin did this because, as she said in the film, "If we are going to eat them, we at least owe them some respect."[5]

The HBO film *Temple Grandin* illuminated Grandin's challenges in being heard and accepted by cattle ranchers. In the beginning, many cattlemen couldn't relate to her sensitivity and didn't believe in her gifts of knowing how cattle felt, so they laughed at her and quickly disregarded her insights. Many told her the building of this new slaughterhouse would be too expensive. They also had doubts that the changes she proposed in the environment where the cattle lived, including the slaughterhouse, would make any difference in the well-being of the cattle. Over years of persistence and patience, Grandin tenaciously and repeatedly did whatever it took to continually expose her ideas and blueprints to cattle ranchers. Her cattle living systems and slaughterhouses are now being used for half of the cattle handled in the United States.[6]

In addition to this, I think it's important that we reconsider the methods we use to perform the act of slaughter. When it comes to the suffering of animals and the subsequent quality of meat we consume, we need to do more studies on the effects of captive bolt stunning and other methods such as Kosher and Halal that are used in commercial facilities, particularly when machines are involved in the slaughter process. There is little research available, and the research I've reviewed showed contradictory results of whether animals experience pain during captive bolt stunning, Halal, and Kosher methods. When I connect to the horse and nature spirits on this issue, my intuitive feeling is that the majority of slaughter that currently occurs in our world is not done humanely.

In the meantime, there is more we can do to adequately prepare the animals, to lessen the suffering they experience when they are taken on a different routine that day—death. It would be beneficial to connect to an animal's Divine Self before the death will take place, thereby showing respect and honor for the sacred exchange of their life in return for our sustenance. We could ask this aspect of an animal's being to bring forth into their awareness the imminence of their death. The Divine Self of each animal will relay this information to the animal's consciousness in a way they can comprehend, helping them in the process of death by allowing them to more easily and quickly surrender and exit their bodies, perhaps even before the act of slaughter occurs.

We can also call upon the help of the nature spirits. As well as grounding and maintaining an animal's life force, they can also assist in death, by extinguishing their energies in the most natural, calming way. Mother Nature has the ability to create life, and can just as easily take it away. This is reflected in the cycles of life and death that we see around us each day, even in the obvious changes of season. If we can properly use more humane methods of slaughter, work with the animal's Divine Self, and ask for the assistance of nature, the whole process doesn't have to be cruel and traumatizing.

MYSTERY AND MAGIC

During the several months I spent discovering the enchantment of wild horses, farm animals, and nature, things remained uncertain between Brian and me. We were still just friends, but I could feel the bond and connection strengthen between us through the depth of our conversations, and the way he opened up more to me with each passing day.

I taught him what I knew spiritually, and gave him energetic tools to use to shift out of the depression and confusion that had taken over most of his adult life. He eagerly absorbed this knowledge and expressed his desire to continue learning. He also began to be curious about his future in a way he never considered before. Without trying to, I received information from the nature spirits who were as much my guides these days as the horse spirits.

They told me Brian's purpose was with agriculture, and in particular, helping to heal Mother Earth. His healing would positively impact the level of abundance and quality of goods that she supplies for all who live on her—the food, clothing, and shelter materials, the foundations of technology, and all that we use in our daily lives. He would also be involved in educating humanity about our role in maintaining these valuable resources. By the time I revealed this information to him, he was already beginning to realize it himself.

When we had time off together, Brian and I would spend it hiking, meditating in nature, or soaking in the hot springs of Ojai. There we would commune with the nature spirits and devas. It was always a transformational experience. The time we spent in nature together gave me a sense of empowerment, motivation, and inspiration on my path, and Brian reported feeling extra grounded, supported, and safe.

We also performed ceremonies in the areas we felt drawn to in nature, especially creeks, forests, and rocky deserts. I knew that, individually and together, we had what the nature spirits called "energetic data" that would benefit humanity and living beings in the world. With our intent and willingness, we began the ceremonies by holding hands. This physical connection is what allowed the energy to move through our bodies and out our chakras into areas of the nature kingdom and Earth. Whether it was healing for a mountain, tree, or a field of crops, I knew the energy that moved through us together was more powerful than for either of us alone.

I was grateful for the power and encouragement I received when we communed with nature because things weren't going completely the way I had planned for being able to quit my hospital job. Although there was an increase in my private clientele, it wasn't enough to be able to support myself financially. I also hadn't attracted the number of horse clients I expected in the area, but at least I was now actively doing the Equine Facilitated Learning (EFL) work with a colleague who had horses.

Despite many of the obstacles that were still on my path, I was happy with the progress I had made working in the EFL field, which had taken me close to five years to get going. I had come a long way since starting this vocation with the workshop horses from New Jersey, and was relieved to finally discover there were many horses out there—privately owned and rescued— who were willing to be involved and highly competent in this healing work with humans. I knew building up clientele took time, persistence, and patience. I was willing to hang in there for the long haul, but I also began to question the guidance of the horse spirits. After all, they were the ones who called me to Ojai to reach horse owners. Did I misunderstand?

Then one day, my whole world turned upside down. Brian called to let me know he had decided to go back to school to study agriculture. He was inspired and motivated to make the changes needed to heal, grow, and move into his soul's purpose, and he was thankful for all my help along the way. I remember he told me he owed me, and that he would make it up to me somehow, someday. But he had to move up north to go to school. He had to focus on his studies. He agreed to stay in touch, but for now we would be parting ways.

I was filled with joy, pride, and sorrow all at once. I was glad to hear that he had finally realized his purpose, and that he would make something of his life. I knew deep down that he needed to go up north, get away, and get through this part of his path on his own. But at the same time, I was losing him. How could this be happening again? My mind clutched at possible potentials—perhaps we could stay in touch frequently, even visit each other from time to time, maintaining our relationship. My heart sank still, because I knew there was no guarantee. We weren't even in a relationship yet.

The hardest part for me was what I already knew but could not tell. Supplementing what my guides had conveyed earlier, the nature spirits confirmed that he was indeed another soul-mate, and still a potential partner in this reality. They went on further to explain that he was also a soul aspect. When they said soul aspect, they meant that we were like petals from the same flower. My soul and his, together with many others, made up a larger soul group. In addition to this, we are polar opposites. Brian and I hold contrasting gender energies at the soul group level, which explains the magnetic attraction we have, the longing we often feel to be close to one another when apart, and how content we feel when in each other's presence. This serenity is related to a certain level of wholeness achieved when our souls are in close proximity.

At this time in history, part of our task as humans during the shift in consciousness on Earth is to move beyond gender, discovering and embracing our feminine and masculine sides in a balanced way. Brian and I are role models in the world for this new, balanced human, as we both are more easily accepting and exhibiting our masculine and feminine sides. Although I am assertive, active, and multi-tasking, I am also very intuitive, open, and receptive. Brian is sensitive, emotional and artistic, but also incredibly grounded and supportive.

I could now see and understand that there were opportunities for us to co-create together, Brian in farming, and myself with the animals. It was the coming together of two humans who equally express the masculine and feminine energies, opposing soul aspects that when adjoined, radiate a greater wholeness into the world. This consequential harmony released into the human, animal, and nature kingdoms could evoke great healing and transformation. As we followed our inner calling and utilized our talents, a flourishing bounty and beauty, and the assistance in bringing forth a healthy co-existence for all living beings could result. With my psychic vision, I saw us beginning our work, a small homestead farm with animals. We could—we would!—show others the way through our example.

And then I finally discovered what had long eluded me—the reason why my horse healing work hadn't taken off yet. My life had indeed gone in a different direction since I left the ranch and met Brian. I was being asked to work with horses and farm animals, with nature as my guide. As I had become more deeply connected to nature, all aspects that made up nature's healing power—the spirits, devas, and Earth—wanted to weave their energies through me while I provided my healing services. My future with horses was awaiting the implementation of this new style of healing. It also dawned on me that the readiness of the recipients of this healing—not just the horses, but their humans as well—was still in progress. This was another reason for the delay, and yet the nature spirits insisted that I continue to be patient.

My guides let me know that if this was goodbye with Brian, there would be another coming into my life very soon. I no longer had to learn lessons about self-love, attachment, and desire the hard way. I passed the tests I went through with Dan. And so I knew, from deep within my core, that this next relationship would be so much easier to get started. It would progress in a completely different way.

Although I felt relief with all of this future information, I was still heartbroken about Brian. A part of me felt I needed to grieve the loss, but I didn't know how things would turn out with him yet. Could we really have a long distance, casual relationship over four years while he finished school? I knew there was still a chance for us to be a couple someday, but I didn't know if it was wise to wait for someone again. I spent two months vacillating between loss and hope. It was a dreary, fretful time. I felt alone yet free, lost in the void between the past and the unforeseeable future. It was as if the time we spent together hadn't even happened, although the sorrow and joy that I carried reminded me that it had.

I reached out to the people I loved and trusted, and recovered immensely after spending time with a powerful local healer who worked with groups. Because of the potency that comes with group energy, the healing was ten or twenty times stronger than it would have been if I had received it individually. I felt comforted and supported throughout the devastating, intense pain of loss again. I turned to nature for help, and was not let down by the gentle, soothing forces that cleared lifetimes of loss with Brian. Although we had loved many times before, we had certainly lost each other just as often.

After a few months that felt like years, I made a decision for myself that I simply had to let him go. I needed to make a clean break for my own sanity, and so I could have the chance to start over with someone new. I also didn't want to get in his way. I knew he needed to make a change in his life, and I didn't want to influence his decision either way. Only he could decide what was best for him.

A few weeks after deciding to let him go, with my heart on the mend, I awoke from a dream. In it, I had just sent in a letter of resignation to my manager at work. I was traveling all over the world speaking on behalf of the rights and freedom of animals, and teaching animal communication and healing classes. I was on top of the world. I couldn't remember a time in my life where I felt this elated. As I reflected on this dream, I knew it was time to quit my job. Although it didn't look like I had enough clients to make as much money as I did at the hospital, I knew that I would find a way.

That week, I analyzed my financial situation. I looked at how much I had coming in and going out, without the hospital salary. I had a chunk of money in savings that could potentially last about eight months. There were also expenses that I could avoid or eliminate from my life. Later that same week, I ran into two psychic acquaintances I knew from the community who asked me if I had quit my job yet. They both shared that it seemed like it was already done. This validating synchronicity was an important catalyst that helped me take a leap of faith. I went for it!

I planned to wait until after the holidays to give my two weeks' notice. It felt right to make a dramatic change like this at the beginning of a new year. Although I was anxious about the uncertainty of my future career and money, the process of leaving a profession I had worked in for thirteen years was remarkably easy and graceful. I knew the timing was right. On my last day of work, my co-workers threw me a goodbye party. Things couldn't have ended on a better note.

For weeks after leaving my job, I felt a liberty and lightness that lifted my soul out of the well of despair where it had plummeted when I lost Brian. I still believed anything was possible when it came to love. I decided to follow up on the counsel of my dream, and began teaching animal communication and healing classes at local boarding facilities, rescues, and metaphysical bookstores. "The magic is about to begin," my guides whispered to me.

CHAPTER TWELVE

ANIMAL COMMUNICATION AND HEALING: AN OVERVIEW

I have spent many years listening to and understanding the subtleties of the personalities and energy systems of horses and other animals. Over time, I've discovered new ways to communicate with these highly sensitive and psychic beings on a deeper level, and ways to work with energy so as to benefit their lives on a body, mind, and spirit level. It is my intent to pass this information on so horse and other animal owners can finally see the life changes they have desired for their animals. For the purposes of this book, I will reference horses when sharing the following information, but all of these ideas and skills can be applied to any animal or aspect of nature.

This chapter gives an overview of animal communication and healing in a simple, step-by-step process. For those who are looking for more in-depth information, activities for practicing, or advanced skills (such as healing with aspects of nature, color, and light) in an extensive format, I am currently in the process of putting together *For the Love of Horses: An Animal*

Communication and Healing Workbook. When completed, this workbook will be a tool and guide for animal communication workshop participants and those who wish to expand their innate intuitive abilities.

When learning the basic skills of animal communication and healing start off by asking open-ended questions and making direct requests. This will assist you in discovering the unique language of your intuition—deciphering the symbols, images, words, feelings, and physical sensations that are involved in this natural approach.

First of all, as I have already mentioned in this book, it is important to be aware of the fact that a human's energy greatly affects a horse's behavior and well-being, both in and out of the saddle. Authors Linda Kohanov and Wyatt Webb have explained and given examples to illustrate this point in their books. If a human is feeling anxious, ungrounded, insecure, angry, or stressed, the horse will pick up on it and often act it out. This is the basis for behaviors such as pacing in stalls, running away when you want to halter them, and bolting off, rearing up, or bucking. Therefore, becoming calm, centered, and grounded is a primary step to take before any interaction with your horse is attempted—whether it's to communicate, heal, do ground work, make a visit to their stall, or take them out to ride.

A simple technique for getting grounded quickly is to take a few deep belly breaths, bring your awareness into the present moment, and imagine that your body's aura (the energy field around you) contains a magnet that is attracted to Earth's iron core. You should instantly feel more centered. While in the process of getting grounded and calm, especially with the hectic schedules and lives we all lead, instead of stuffing thoughts, emotions, or physical sensations, or trying to force them out of your mind and body, simply notice them. Before heading off to your horse, take a moment to do the self-awareness check-in that I described in Chapter Five, based on Kohanov's body scan from *Riding Between the Worlds*. Tune in to your body from head to toe to become aware of what is going on in each area.

During this process, a certain area of your body might light up or stand out to you, signaling a need for consideration. You could start there and work your way around your whole body. The entire method takes only a few minutes. As you focus on each body area, you may receive information in the form of physical sensations (such as pain or pressure), emotions, thoughts or words, pictures, colors, or even symbols. Simply be present with what you receive for another minute more.

In the second part of the self-awareness check-in, you'll get more clarity about the information you are receiving. Tune in to your Divine Self, which lies within the light that runs through the core of your body. It is easiest to access from the heart chakra, but can be accessed from any chakra in the body. As you bring your focus on the light that lies within your heart chakra, you will connect to your Divine Self. As you make contact, ask this part of your being for more information or greater clarity. If you're adequately connected, the information you now receive should make more sense. It should either provide a precise answer, or an expanded form of the original word, color, emotion, or sensation.

As you remain present, the sensations, thoughts, or emotions should lighten or shift, allowing you to feel more centered, calm, and grounded. At this point, even if you are still very aware of your internal experience, it is safe to spend time with your horse, because it's unlikely he will act out your energies now that you are actively processing them through your awareness.

This is also the first step in beginning to communicate with your horse. Once you have received information about what is going on within you, you are now opened up to access information about what is going on with your horse. As you interact with your horse throughout all the activities you do together, you might have questions for him or her. Perhaps you want to know how he is feeling today or why he went around the jump in the arena instead of over it.

To ask these questions, imagine sending those thoughts or words from your mind to the center of your horse's forehead. With your intent, this energy transmission will occur. You can also relay a message to your horse about what you would like him to do; for example, by visualizing an image of the horse going over the jump in the arena and then sending him the picture. Sending images gives you the best chance at success, because animals think primarily in pictures. At the same time that you send this information to your horse, speak the questions or requests out loud. As Marta Williams shared in her book *Beyond Words: Talking with Animals and Nature*, this is a good way to back up your message. If your horse has fully received your question and request he will lick and chew. Give him a few moments to do this, as sometimes there is a delay because he is processing the information.

In addition, you can send your horse feedback, energy, or emotions exactly the same way as you did with the questions and requests above. If you want your horse to back up out of your space, send the picture of what you want him to do from your mind to his, say the words out loud, and send a line of energy out from your aura to his. You can emphasize this message if you send the energy out from your solar plexus chakra, the "power" chakra located between your rib cage and navel. You can also send love, gratitude, or joy from your heart to his, or wherever you sense that emotion originates in your body. Send the words of any feedback you would like to give him, from your mind to his.

After you have sent your question or message to your horse telepathically, through this mind-to-mind transmission, you can now open up to receive his response. He might have already demonstrated this for you, through his actions. If you asked him to eat his food or take his medicine and he's following through, you've achieved your goal.

But if you've asked him a question, there is still more work to do. The easiest way to receive messages is by tuning in to your body again, this time with the reverse intention of communicating with your horse. As I learned in Eve Lee's workshop Horses As Mirrors of Our Souls, you can use your body as a sensing tool for understanding what is going on with your horse. I will take that a step further and add that you can use your body as a receptor for your horse's messages. Since you have already tuned in to your body before interacting with your horse, you know what is going on with you. This is an important step that helps prevent confusing your own internal messages with your horse's messages.

Face your horse and go within, focusing on each body part again, with special emphasis on the area in the center of your brain. This is where the pineal gland, also known as your intuitive center, is located. What do you feel, sense, see, hear, or know, as you tune in to each body area? Do you receive a picture, word, sound, color, or symbol?

Your spirit guides will be helping you in the process of translating the energy of your animal's messages, which will take a form that is easiest for you to understand. For this reason it's important to follow your first hit or inclination, and not doubt or dismiss what you intuit. If you are confused by what you receive, ask your Divine Self for more clarity.

If you received the same information about your horse that you received when you checked in with yourself in the beginning, it can mean that you both are experiencing something similar. But it usually means that one of you, either you or your horse, is empathically picking up the other's energy. When you get to the healing section of this chapter, you will find information about how you can clear these empathic energies. It's a good idea to get in the habit of clearing these energies on a regular basis, because empathic sensitivity is commonly experienced in bonded humans and animals and can lead to emotional distress or health problems.

If you asked your horse how he was doing today and received a picture of him running and bucking as he does when he is turned out and having a good time, you can assume the picture means he is well, or even that he'd like to do this now. Let's stick with our example and say you asked why he didn't go over the jump in the arena. If you received a picture of his feet, or the words "it hurts," or got a physical sensation of pain in your feet or another area of your body, that is your answer. Begin checking in with his feet, or another area of his body that you picked up on. Is he sore? Did he have new shoes placed recently, or is there something else wrong?

If you envision him involved in another activity or being back in his stall eating, is it possible he could be bored, tired, hungry, or all three of these? You would follow this same procedure for any other kind of information you might receive, unraveling all of the mysteries of your horse, like a detective who interprets clues and evidence to solve a crime.

If you want to receive more information about how your horse is doing overall, how you can care for him better, or how to improve his health and well-being, you might want to also connect to the horse deva and his nature spirit for additional advice. To do this, get grounded and centered as I described at the beginning of this section. Then, with your intent, ask to connect to the horse deva or his nature spirit (the energy that assists his physical body functioning). If you wish to contact both of them, connect to each of them separately. When you do this, you should notice a shift in how your body feels; perhaps you become aware of a change in your energy, an emotion, vision, or another physical sensation. Machaelle Small Wright discussed this process in her book *Behaving As If the God in All Life Mattered.* This new sensation and awareness is your cue that you've made contact.

After contact is initiated, ask for the information you desire the same way you did when communicating with your animal, as I described above—through sending thoughts, words, pictures, emotions, or energy. Ask very specific questions if you want to receive detailed answers. Then open up to receive the horse deva and nature spirit's response. Again, use the same techniques I gave you above for receiving messages from your horse.

The protocols I have offered are just tools. They are helpful in the beginning for the basics and essence of animal communication. It takes lots of practice, dedication, additional skills through more training, classes, or study—and experience that unfolds over a period of time—to feel confident in this kind of ability. I encourage you to use these tools as guidelines, and to be open to discovering how to work uniquely with your own intuition. You might find that when you are completely present, open, and unbiased with an animal, the communication happens for you in a completely original manner. Trust this, follow it, and see where it leads.

It's important to know that it takes time to fully trust the information you receive. This is a huge part of being successful at this work as well, even if you're only doing it to understand your animals better. If you don't trust yourself, you won't want to know certain things or you will discount much of the information you receive, thinking it couldn't possibly be true. Learning to trust—and healing any self-trust that has been lost due to life traumas—is part of the journey for many healers and psychics. This is especially true for those of us who were not believed, understood, or validated for our gifts growing up. Our current, masculine-dominated society still does not completely support one's choice to honor and follow their intuition. Despite this challenge, some of the most successful psychics I know are those who were never afraid to be wrong. Their careers had many ups and downs, but they never gave up and worked to continue to overcome their own self-doubt.

TECHNIQUES FOR ENERGY HEALING AND CLEARING

Once you have deepened the connection with your horse through sending and receiving messages, you can then practice basic healing techniques. When it comes to working with energy to help your horse, it is of utmost importance to be dedicated to your own personal growth and development. Even highly trained and experienced horse people will have issues with horses from time to time if they are not aware of and actively healing their own core issues or life challenges. Become aware of your weaknesses when you tune in to your body in the procedure I explained in the section above. Then follow up by participating in activities that help you become stronger, whether it is through meditation, yoga, energy healing, psychotherapy, or any kind of healing or spiritual practice that feels right to you, whether alternative or mainstream in origin.

Many behavior and riding challenges arise due to issues with control, power, trust, and boundaries. Our horses often have life challenges that mirror our own. When you gain a certain level of personal mastery in these problem areas, you will naturally carry this mastery in your aura. Thereafter, every time you have contact with your horse, you will influence him for the better. As you develop more self-control, self-trust, empowerment, and healthy boundaries in your own life, your horse will respond more appropriately by cooperating, trusting you, following your lead, and respecting your space. When it comes to unwavering emotional or behavioral issues and physical illness, it helps to use some hands-on techniques.

Many of us are natural healers, and the chakras or energy centers in our hands are already opened and ready for use. If you are not sure, with your intent, connect to your Divine Self as described in the communication procedure above, and ask that the hand chakras be opened and made ready for healing. We are living in a time when potent, transformative energies that can assist us in healing and thriving are readily available to us through the universal energy that naturally runs through our bodies. We don't have to alter our consciousness through trance states, consumption of drugs or other substances, chanting, or other spiritual practices to access them as we have for thousands of years. We can simply call forth and utilize these healing energies for optimum results in health and wellness. As long as our intention is for the highest good of our horses, the energy will help and never harm.

To access the universal flow, tune in to the area just above your head, your eighth chakra. Ask that the current, healing energies appropriate for your animal be downloaded into the energy centers of your body. As these centers are filled up, you are ready for hands-on work. Through the power of your intent and willingness, lay your hands on any area of your horse's body that carries illness, pain, or emotional suffering.

Connect to your Divine Self again and ask that your animal only receive the amount of healing that is appropriate for him today, and that is in alignment with his soul's desire. This will prevent him from receiving more energy than he is able to integrate at one time. You will also be complying with the karmic law of honoring one's free will.

Now you are ready to begin. The healing energies within the life force energy that is now flowing through your body's energy centers will exit your hands and enter your horse's body. You will notice that your hands begin to feel hot, or cool and tingly. Either one is appropriate. Keep your hands in that area, until the hot or cool sensation diminishes or disappears, or until you've been doing the healing for at least fifteen minutes. Stay as present as you can, so the healing energies will channel efficiently by the power of your focus. If your horse becomes restless or moves away after some time has passed, it is also a sign that the healing is complete.

When you finish, tune in to your eighth chakra and ask for a flush of universal energy to clear all of your energy fields and your physical body. You can also tune in to your Divine Self and ask for assistance in clearing out these energies. In either case, you should notice a shift in energy. Thereafter, any energies that you have picked up from your horse through the healing process will be released. This part of hands-on work is very important, because you don't want to take on emotional or physical imbalances that can cause distress and illness.

In reverse, if you sense that your horse has empathically picked up your energies—thoughts, emotions, body sensations or illness, whether during this healing or in everyday living—you can connect to his Divine Self by tuning in to the light deep within his heart chakra. As you make contact, you should again notice a shift in energy. Then make the request that his Divine Self clear these energies from all of his energy fields and his physical body. Continue to hold the connection with his Divine Self until the process is complete, which may take anywhere from a few moments up to a minute or so.

A shift in energy, the desire to take a deep breath, or the urge to get up and move, is your cue that the energy has cleared. Keep in mind, though, that depending on your horse's level of consciousness, he might pick these energies right back up again and carry them in his energy fields or his physical body. You can work with his Divine Self to continue clearing his fields as many times a day as needed, but ultimately, his soul makes the final decision.

Similar to energy healing modalities such as Reiki or Pranic Healing, the hands-on technique I described above works with the universal life force energy that surrounds and runs through our bodies. The technique I offer differs in that it involves specifically calling forth the upgraded, healing energies available in this dimension since the late 1990s. As I've explained above, you channel these energies through the chakras in your hands while touching the appropriate body area.

This is unlike many other energy healing modalities that do not use a hands-on approach. These transmutative energies will move through your chakras within the universal energy flow, the sustaining life force energy that promotes wellness. You should also be aware that while providing healing, these energies will exit all of your chakras, not just your hand chakras.

In fact, you don't even have to use your hands at all. If this is your intention, connect to your Divine Self, and ask that the energy emanate from your being, which is the basis for how most distance energy healing operates (distance energy healing being healing that does not require the recipient to be where the healer is physically located at the time the healing occurs). Energy instantly goes wherever it is directed; it follows intent. This is a universal law and the basis for explanations on how our own thoughts, emotions, and energy create our personal realities, as well as affect the lives of everyone we come into contact with. *Energy Medicine: The Scientific Basis,* by James Oschman, and *The Energy Healing Experiments: Science Reveals Our Natural Power to Heal,* by Gary E. Schwartz, revealed the scientific facts, further describing how in-person and distance energy healing occurs, as well as uncovering documented research to prove how this type of healing benefits the lives of all who receive it.

Other healing resources available in the universal energy flow include sacred geometry. Sacred geometry refers to naturally occurring geometric configurations or shapes that can help us heal, manifest intentions, and develop personal mastery. They are called sacred because nature is comprised of these foundational, archetypal patterns. They are a universal, non-denominational access to spirituality and wellness. Drunvalo Melchizedek's book *The Ancient Secret of the Flower of Life, Vol. 1* expanded on this idea and provided detailed information and more advanced ways to work with sacred geometry.

For beginners, I recommend following this basic protocol for working with sacred geometry: with your intent, connect to your Divine Self and ask that the appropriate sacred geometric structures be placed in the right area of your horse's energy field, for assistance with mastering a life lesson, such as love, trust, empowerment, control, or boundaries. You can repeat this procedure to heal yourself, and also be a better role model for your horse.

You don't have to be specific about the amount or type of geometric structures you are invoking, only the lessons that you are learning. Through the power of your intent, aligned with the universal laws, your verbal request is enough to bring forth the structures that will benefit your life or your horse's life. Once again, ask that your animal only receive the amount of healing that is appropriate for him today, and that is in alignment with his soul's desire.

You can also ask that the appropriate sacred geometric shapes be placed for physical healing in a particular body area. A couple minutes after your request, you should feel a shift within yourself, like a rush of energy, or a warm or cool sensation. Or you might feel sleepy, notice your body moves into a specific posture, or even feel a slowing or deepening of your breathing. You might also notice your horse begin to lick, chew, breathe deeply, transfer his weight to the other side of his body, or walk away, signaling that the shift has occurred. However you sense the shift is perfectly appropriate and unique to you as a healer.

When you work with sacred geometry, you can place your hands on an area of your animal where you sense that shift is needed, but a hands-on approach is not necessary. Like the procedure I discussed above for channeling the healing energies in the universal flow, you can just connect to your Divine Self, ask for the healing, and expect that it will occur. Unlike channeling the transformative energies, you won't invoke the sacred geometric shapes into your body (unless you are doing this healing on yourself) or radiate them from your being, but simply ask that they be directed into your horse's body or energy field. Again, you should feel a shift within yourself, or notice a shift has occurred by your horse's behavior.

You cannot do the above techniques incorrectly. If you don't feel any sensations in your hands or notice a shift within yourself or your horse, you probably haven't fully connected to your Divine Self or allowed the download of the healing energies. You also must be grounded, centered, and in the present moment to work with any of these energies, including sacred geometry, or it can be more difficult to access or invoke them. Remember that these are basic techniques, merely an introduction to healing, but a good place to start. I've studied and worked with them since I've begun my healing and spiritual journey. I now work with a variety of eclectic energy modalities, but they are well beyond the scope of this book.

Most healing is a gradual process for each living being, and each soul chooses how much healing they want to receive at one time. As a healer, you can only direct the energies, or be a vessel for the transmission of them. It is not up to you to change or cure your horse. If you pick up on resistance from your horse, you can connect to their Divine Self and ask this aspect of their being, if it's appropriate, to help them become ready and willing to receive and integrate the healing. Sometimes it is just not the time or way that a horse's soul prefers to heal. It is also essential that you get permission—non-verbally from your own horse, and verbally from another animal's human if you decide to help other animals—before doing the healing. Get verbal permission if you work with humans, as these techniques can be used for us as well.

In addition, the animal communication skills, healing techniques, and health guidelines I've shared in this book should never be a substitute for diagnosis and treatment with a licensed medical professional or veterinarian for any physical or mental health issues in humans or animals. This book is not a certification course, and does not legally entitle you to provide professional intuitive and healing services with humans or animals. The information, skills, and techniques in this chapter are offered for the benefit of you and your animal.

After gaining more experience, training, and/or certification beyond the scope of this book, if you want to begin a career in healing, follow all laws in your state, county, or province regarding the legality of any hands-on modalities. In some states, you must be a licensed professional, such as a medical doctor, massage therapist, or veterinarian to do certain kinds of hands-on healing with humans or animals. For more information about the laws in your state, county, or province, contact your Attorney General, or an attorney who specializes in medical or animal law.

No matter whom you work with, if it is their intent to heal, they will receive a shift, even if it's hardly noticeable to you. We are living in a time where rapid healing and transformation is possible for many. Substantial progress can be made in shorter periods of time, unlike a decade or two ago. For this reason, I recommend that you repeat these healing techniques as often as you think it is necessary. For pain issues, they can be done two times daily; for disease, at least once a day; and for emotional and behavioral issues, once or twice a week is a general guideline.

When it comes to tuning in to your body and connecting to your Divine Self to send and receive messages to and from your horses, and working with the healing energies within the universal flow and sacred geometry, nothing leads to success overnight. Miracles do happen, and should be expected. But like many life challenges and goals, it usually takes time, energy, dedication, patience, and persistence to experience major change on a body, mind, or spirit level. It is also essential that you get to the root cause of many emotional disturbances, physical illnesses, or behavioral issues, or they may recur, even if you've seen a decrease or elimination of symptoms since the healing.

Continue to use these communication skills and energy techniques on a regular basis for the best results. Each time we open up the lines of communication with our horses through practice in sending and receiving messages, and through working with energy, we are connecting with them on a deeper level. This connection allows us to better understand them, helps them respond to us quicker and easier, and gives us more information about how we can help them heal, as well as how to heal ourselves in the process.

CHAPTER THIRTEEN

MIRACLES AND MOVEMENT

Over the next few months after quitting my job, besides teaching animal and nature communication classes, I did more EFL work with adults, and even taught horse communication classes to children, helping them learn and discover all there is to know about the behavior, body parts, and language of horses. My healing business started to pick up. I also got a job offer as an on-site animal caretaker.

I considered this opportunity, which would have included feeding, grooming, exercising, and administering medications to horses, as well as other farm animals. As I looked into this offer and others that involved on-site work with farm animals or farming in general, I realized most of them didn't feel quite right. Either I would have to share private living space with someone, or it was too far from where I was currently living, or it would take too much time away from my other healing endeavors.

I wanted to work for someone who valued the time, energy, and gifts I would bring to their animals, someone who, in addition to the psychic information and energy healing I provided, would also appreciate any extra time I spent riding, caring for them, or just being in their presence. Not only would this be enjoyable for me, but it would benefit their horses as well. This is true for any other kind of healer, caretaker, pet sitter, trainer, or farrier. The more time and TLC they give to the animals, the more they can provide guidance and comfort, maintain health, and strengthen the human-animal bond.

In addition, all healers carry a high vibration in their energy fields, which is the basis for how they heal. This doesn't mean that healers have fully mastered every aspect of human existence or that they don't have challenging days or issues that can decrease their vibration. It does mean that when taking into consideration all aspects of their being and areas of their lives, in order to provide the greatest benefit to others, healers must regularly emanate an overall higher vibration than those they work with.

To explain this further, according to the law of attraction, any lower vibrations while in the presence of higher vibrations will be inclined to rise into a higher vibration, with positive effects. This can happen when the human or animal holding an overall lower vibration, due to any number of reasons, including illness, makes any kind of contact with the healer, for example, by being in close physical proximity, reading their work, or even visiting their website. They don't need to book a session with the healer, and the healer doesn't need to have the intent of healing, for this to occur.

In this way, many humans and animals are given opportunities to shift and grow, without even being aware of it. On an unconscious level, however, they will decide if or to what extent they will allow the healing energy to raise them up. In certain cases, if the human or animal rejects the healing energy, they will usually avoid the healer as well, and the pull into a higher vibration. But frequently the opposite happens, and humans and animals are attracted to the healing energy.

I used to ride with a friend named Lucy who lived in the Santa Barbara area. She had two horses who behaved as if they had some heavy traumas from their pasts. They were what many horse people would call "old, broke" horses, who would submit to your every command, never flinch or resist, no matter how restricting the bit or girth, or how hard you pulled on the reins. In fact, Lucy referred to them as bomb-proof, meaning that if a bomb were to go off nearby, they wouldn't move a muscle, much less spook. She reported to me that many times while riding or preparing to ride, especially if she used extra force or pressure while saddling them, or when she was nervous, they would respond by lowering their heads in defeat, with eyes glazed over. It sounded like dissociation to me.

Fortunately, I had the opportunity to ride both of her horses. I didn't know anything about their pasts, and I didn't do any healing work with them intentionally. But during the times I rode them, they both seemed to come alive. As they picked up the pace while I was on their backs, I felt an excitement brewing in them below me. Lucy said they never acted like this before. They were always slow, plodding along, and it was often hard to get them going. Even weeks later, she reported that there was a brightness and presence in their eyes that she had never seen. She felt they were different somehow, but couldn't pinpoint it. Mostly, she was glad they seemed to enjoy riding more.

I'm not surprised by these experiences, because healing does not have to occur in a formal way. As I sat on top of each horse, I made direct contact with their solar plexus chakra, located in the middle of their back. Traumas that have to do with disempowerment are often held in the solar plexus area, so it makes sense that with riding, the position was right for a release.

In addition to healing trauma, when I ride horses or give them extra care and attention, it can help me become aware of anything I wouldn't normally notice during everyday chores. This can help prevent the development of an illness or emotional issue, or give me the opportunity to intervene at an earlier stage for a more successful outcome. Like the experience I had with Lucy's horses, interacting with and riding horses can clarify what their life has been like with other humans, and how riding has been for them. Many horses develop defense mechanisms to deal with what is going on in their life, including riding, and these can easily be seen and healed if I'm given the time and opportunity to experience them.

Even though I did not accept an animal caretaker position, I was happy with the direction my work was taking—and my life. Looking back, I realized that if I hadn't had such a delay in getting started with the EFL work, I wouldn't have had the opportunity to implement my intuitive-healing abilities, and it is those abilities that have enabled me to help many animals and humans in unexpected ways. I was grateful for the calling of the dream horses years before, because I had come full circle in my destiny. I loved the land I lived on, and was enjoying the new community I was part of. During this time, I also formed a solid network of friends I resonated with, who had similar goals and dreams. It was the beginning of the spiritual support I had longed for almost a decade before.

It seemed that I had gotten over Brian; or at least when I thought of him, I didn't feel the familiar pangs of loss and hurt, longing or regret. And then, like Dorothy waking up in Oz, one day a new life began for me. I remember the sweet, comforting sentiments as if it was yesterday. It began like a normal Saturday. Having the day to myself, I was relaxing, listening to the quiet sounds of nature playing on a CD at home. I began to think about what the nature spirits had told me before I quit my job: "That's when the magic happens." The doorbell rang. I wondered who it was; I wasn't expecting anyone.

To my astonishment when I answered the door, there standing before me was Brian. With a sheepish smile and cheeks flushed in self-consciousness, he began to speak slowly. My heart beat with excitement and nervous anticipation. I was still trying to make sense of what I was seeing and what was happening. Could it really be true that he was here? Should I pinch myself to make sure I wasn't dreaming?

He told me he had changed his mind about school. He told me he didn't want to live away from me. He told me (and it took me a good hour to fully process this one) that he wanted to be with me. He had made his decision. My jaw dropped to my knees. I couldn't believe it and yet I could. Somewhere deep inside, I had known this would happen all along. We sure had a lot to talk about. I had many questions that needed answering.

So we took the time to talk that day, ironing out everything that had happened between us, what made him originally want to be apart from me, including his desire to go to school. Although he really wanted to do school, he decided he was better at the experiential process of gardening and farming. Besides, he had plenty of experience under his belt already, beyond this lifetime.

If I told you everything that we went through since then, I would have to write another book. I will say that we made a decision to begin a relationship that day. And being in a relationship with Brian was a testament to the serious self-healing I had committed myself to for over a decade. There was a time in my life when attracting in a man who is kind, loving, with whom I share common goals and dreams, and am able to be intimate with, would not have been possible. Over the course of the following year we continued to heal ourselves individually, as well as deal with the issues that were shown to us through the mirror of our relationship. And we still do. Like many couples, we have ups and downs, but we are courageous enough to see ourselves through it all. Since the time we finally got together, we have developed a stronger relationship, one that continues to help us grow, evolve, and love each other even more.

We lived in Ojai together for several months, and then our life path shifted course and we found ourselves in Arizona. The nature spirits were right. If we ended up together, our lives would completely change. We lived in a rural area on the outskirts of Sedona, Arizona, surrounded by horse pastures and cottonwood trees. Moving there was a great opportunity for both of us, with more options for Brian to do farming and nursery work, and more of a chance for me to continue to build my healing practice.

After Arizona, we spent some time in northern California working on a vegetable, chicken, milking goat, permaculture homestead. We learned more skills in farming there, and continued our spiritual work in healing areas of the Earth together. But ultimately, we were called to California's central coast, and that is where we are today. During the tail end of the publishing process, we moved to Cambria, California. As we give to the central coast in our healing work (Brian's with the Earth in farming, gardening installation and maintenance, and art, and mine with humans, animals, and nature through energy healing), this magical area continues to give back to us in her abundance of community support and restorative, spiritual energy.

It has been quite a mysterious journey and that journey continues, as we get closer to reaching our biggest dreams and goals. We eventually want to have our own farm, with vegetable crops, some farm animals, and horses. As we prepare, we continue to look for opportunities to provide our services on fertile land, learning with other like-minded people who want extra help on their farms, ranches, or healing centers, and where resources and knowledge can be shared.

In the meantime, Brian and I are committed to being in a relationship as long as it is aligned with our highest good. We are continually inspired by the co-creation of our soul's purpose work—the reason we have come together as a couple. Nature thrives on balance. Many aspects of humans and animals are created from nature. Therefore, when we are connected to each other, the wholeness and harmony that resound through our chosen expression of farming and energy healing can benefit Mother Earth and all living beings who live on her. Brian and I are enthusiastic in sharing our message with others about how much the animal and nature kingdoms desire to coexist with us peacefully. Animals and nature wish to be nurtured and cared for, and work with us in a way that can improve our health, wellness, prosperity, and relationships.

THE LOVE CONTINUES
Bringing Change Into Our World

As I have discovered on my long and at times wearisome and uncertain path with the horses, they are our healers and teachers. The horses have been working to help humans for thousands of years. If you have a horse in your life, you can bet there is a deeper reason he or she has come to you, other than your interest in an animal companion or an activity you do together. It is time we all become aware of this, and utilize the wisdom they bring us through being in our lives. It is 2013, the peak time of the great shift in consciousness on planet Earth. This is the right time for humans to pick up the responsibility we have shirked for many centuries.

Do it for the love of horses. Let your love for them kindle the fire of change within you. If we take the time and energy to understand horses, and improve our connection, communication, and relationship with them, we will also be improving their health and well-being. As their health and well-being improves, they are more able to help us heal, evolve, and find inner peace. Like skipping stones across a pond, the ripples from these changes will reach all the beings in our world—other humans, animals, the nature kingdom, and especially Mother Earth herself.

NOTES

CHAPTER ONE—All the Love

1. p. xviii.

2. p. xviii.

3. p. xviii.

4. pp. 152-153.

CHAPTER THREE—What Horses Want

1. p. 23.

2. Stormy May, *The Path of the Horse: Taking The First Step*, Stormy May Productions. 2008, DVD.

3. p. 156.

CHAPTER FOUR—Horses' Medicine

1. Deborah Marshall, MA, Reflection of the Horse (Nanaimo, BC, Canada, Generation Farms, 2008), professional training, p. 16.

2. Eve B. Lee, Horses As Mirrors of Our Souls (Antioch, IL, Equine Magic at Loghaven, July 13-15th, 2007), Equine Facilitated Learning Workshop.

3. p. 64.

4. p. 94.

5. p. 85.

6. p. 51.

7. pp. 96-97.

CHAPTER FIVE—Reconciliation and Rebirth

1. Merriam-Webster Online Dictionary, "Empathy-Medical Definition and More," *Merriam-Webster: An Encyclopedia Britannica Company*, August 6, 2012, http://www. merriam-webster.com/medical/empathy, 2012.

2. pp. 24-25.

3. Deepak Chopra, "Just Listen! Your Body is Speaking To You," *The Huffington Post*, December 23, 2009, http://www.oprah.com/spirit/learn-to-listen-to-Your-Bodys-Signals/2, p. 2.

4. Merriam-Webster Online Dictionary, "Compassion-Merriam-Webster Online," *Merriam-Webster: An Encyclopedia Britannica Company*, September 8, 2012, http://www.merriam-webster. com/dictionary/compassion.

5. p. 19.

CHAPTER SEVEN—The Power of Horse Experience

1. pp. 24-36.

CHAPTER EIGHT—Wild Horse Lessons for Humanity

1. pp. 71, 66 & 70, respectively.

2. p. 28.

3. Mike Cavaroc, "Why America Needs More Predators," *Free Roaming Photography: Wildlife and Nature Photography by Mike Cavaroc,* December, 18, 2012, http://www.blog.freeroamingphotography.com/4800/wildlife/why-america-needs-more-predators.

CHAPTER NINE—A Horse Owner's Responsibility

1. p. 17.

CHAPTER TEN—The Benefits of a Natural Lifestyle

1. *The Animal Rescue Unit: Investigate, Educate, Rehabilitate, and Legislate For Animal Welfare!* "What's Really Happening To American Wild Horses," 2011, http://www.animalrescueunit.com/wildhorsemassacres.htm. p. 1.

2. James Kleinert, *Wild Horses and Renegades: A Modern Day Western,* Director James Kleinert. Moving Cloud Productions. USA, 2010, DVD.

3. p. 109.

CHAPTER ELEVEN—The Teachings of the Nature Spirits

1. p. 120.

2. *The Animal Rescue Unit: Investigate, Educate, Rehabilitate, and Legislate For Animal Welfare!* "What's Really Happening To American Wild Horses," 2011, http://www.animalrescueunit.com/wildhorsemassacres.htm. p. 1.

3. *Animal Law Coalition: Advocating for animals to live and live free of cruelty and neglect,* "U.S. Equine Slaughter Legal Again," November 18, 2011, http://www.animallawcoalition.com/horse-slaughter/article/1887.

4. Evita Ochel, B.Sc., B. Ed., CHN, "15 Reasons Why You May Want to Reconsider Eating Meat," *Evolving Wellness*, April 18, 2009, http://www.evolvingwellness.com/posts/663/15-reasons-why-you-may-want-to-reconsider-eating-meat, #15.

5. Christopher Monger and Merritt Johnson. *Temple Grandin*. Director Mick Jackson. HBO Films. USA, 2010, DVD.

6. Ibid.

BIBLIOGRAPHY AND RESOURCES

Andrews, Ted. *Animal Speak: The Spiritual & Magical Powers of Creatures Great & Small.* St. Paul, MN: Llewellyn Publications, 2003.

Animal Law Coalition: Advocating for animals to live and live free of cruelty and neglect. "U.S. Equine Slaughter Legal Again", November 18, 2011. http://www.animallawcoalition.com/horse-slaughter/article/1887.

Animal Rescue Unit: Investigate, Educate, Rehabilitate, and Legislate For Animal Welfare! "What's Really Happening To American Wild Horses," 2011. http://www.animalrescueunit.com/wildhorsemassa-cres.htm.

Ascended Master El Morya. *The Chela and the Path: Keys to Soul Mastery in the Aquarian Age,* Dictated to the Messenger Elizabeth Clare Prophet. Corwin Springs, MT: Summit University Press, 1976.

Bass, Ellen, and Laura Davis. *The Courage To Heal: A Guide For Women Survivors of Child Sexual Abuse.* Third Edition, Revised and Expanded. New York: HarperCollins, 1994.

Carroll, Lee, and Jan Tober. *The Indigo Children: The New Kids Have Arrived.* Carlsbad, CA: Hay House, Inc., 1999.

Cavaroc, Mike. "Why America Needs More Predators." *Free Roaming Photography: Wildlife and Nature Photography by Mike Cavaroc,* December 18, 2012, http://www.blog.freeroamingphotography.com/4800/wildlife/why-america-needs-more-predators.

Childs, Laura. *The Joy of Keeping Farm Animals: Raising Chickens, Goats, Pigs, Sheep, and Cows.* New York: Skyhorse Publishing, 2010.

Chopra, Deepak. "Just Listen! Your Body is Speaking to You." *The Huffington Post,* December 23, 2009. http://www.oprah.com/spirit/learn-to-listen-to-Your-Bodys-Signals/2.

Choquette, Sonia. *Your Heart's Desire: Instructions for Creating the Life You Really Want.* New York: Three Rivers Press, 1997.

Eden, Donna, with David Feinstein. *Energy Medicine.* New York: Penguin Putnam, Inc., 1998.

Freud, Sigmund. "Jenseits des Lustprinzips." [Beyond the Pleasure Principle] *Internationaler Psychoanalytischer Verlag,* Vienna, 1920.

Fulkerson, Lee. *Forks Over Knives.* Director Lee Fulkerson. Monica Beach Media, Los Angeles, 2011. DVD.

Goleman, Daniel. *Emotional Intelligence: Why It Can Matter More Than IQ.* New York: Bantam Books, 1994.

Grandin, Temple. *Animals in Translation: Using the Mysteries of Autism to Decode Animal Behavior*. Orlando, FL: Harcourt, Inc., 2005.

Hay, Louise. *You Can Heal Your Life*. Carlsbad, CA: Hay House, Inc., 2004.

Hillman, James. *The Soul's Code: In Search of Character and Calling*. New York: Warner Books, 1996.

His Holiness The Dalai Lama. *The Dalai Lama's Book of Love and Compassion*. London: Thorsons, 2011.

Ingerman, Sandra. *Soul Retrieval: Mending the Fragmented Self*. New York: HarperCollins, 1991.

Irwin, Chris. *Horses Don't Lie: What Horses Teach Us About Our Natural Capacity For Awareness, Confidence, Courage, and Trust*. New York: Marlowe & Co., 2001.

Isaacson, Rupert. *Horse Boy: A Father's Quest to Heal His Son*. New York: Little Brown & Co., 2009.

Jackson, Jaime. *The Natural Horse: Foundations For Natural Horsemanship*. Harrison, AR: Star Ridge Publishing, 1992.

Kleinert, James. *Wild Horses and Renegades: A Modern Day Western*. Director James Kleinert. Moving Cloud Productions, USA, 2010. DVD.

Kohanov, Linda. *Riding Between the Worlds: Expanding Our Potential Through the Way of the Horse*. Novato, CA: New World Library, 2003.

_____. *The Tao of Equus: A Woman's Journey of Healing &
Transformation through the Way of the Horse*. Novato, CA: New
World Library, 2001.

Levine, Peter A., with Ann Frederick. *Waking the Tiger: Healing
Trauma*. Berkeley, CA: North Atlantic Books, 1997.

Magdalena, Flo Aeveia. *I Remember Union: The Story of Mary
Magdalena*. New Britain, CT: All Worlds Publishing, 2004.

May, Stormy. *The Path of the Horse: Taking the First Step*. Director
Stormy May. Stormy May Productions, USA, 2008. DVD.

McCormick, Adele Von Rust, Ph.D., Marlena Deborah
McCormick, Ph.D., & Thomas E. McCormick, M.D. *Horses
and the Mystical Path: The Celtic Way of Expanding the Human
Soul*. Novato, CA: New World Library, 2004.

McCormick, Adele Von Rust, Ph.D., and Marlena Deborah
McCormick, Ph.D. *Horse Sense and the Human Heart: What
Horses Teach Us About Trust, Bonding, Creativity, and Spirituality*.
Deerfield, FL: Health Communications, Inc., 1997.

McDougall, John A., M.D. *The McDougall Program: 12 Days To
Dynamic Health*. New York: Penguin Group, 1990.

Melchizedek, Drunvalo. *The Ancient Secret of the Flower of Life*,
Vol. 1. Flagstaff, AZ: Light Publishing Technology, 1998.

Merriam-Webster Online Dictionary. "Compassion-Merriam-
Webster Online," *Merriam-Webster: An Encyclopedia Britannica
Company*, September 8, 2012, http://www.merriam-webster.
com/dictionary/compassion.

_____. "Empathy-Medical Definition and More," *Merriam-Webster: An Encyclopedia Britannica Company*, August 6, 2012, http://www.merriamwebster.com/medical/ empathy.

Miller, Alice. *The Body Never Lies: The Lingering Effects of Cruel Parenting*. New York: W.W. Norton & Co., 2006.

_____. *The Drama of the Gifted Child: The Search For the True Self*. Revised Edition. New York: Basic Books, 1997.

Monger, Christopher, and Merritt Johnson. *Temple Grandin*. Director Mick Jackson. HBO Films, USA, 2010. DVD.

Myss, Caroline. *Sacred Contracts: Awakening Your Divine Potential*. New York: Harmony Books, 2001.

Ochel, Evita, B.Sc., B.Ed., CHN. "15 Reasons Why You May Want to Reconsider Eating Meat." *Evolving Wellness*, April 18, 2009, http://www.evolvingwellness.com/posts/663/15-reasons-why-you-may-want-to reconsider-eating-meat.

Oschman, James L. *Energy Medicine: The Scientific Basis*. London: Churchill Livingstone, 2000.

Peirce, Penny. *Frequency: The Power of Personal Vibration*. New York: Atria Books, 2009.

Pogacnik, Marko. *Nature Spirits & Elemental Beings: Working with the Intelligence in Nature*. Tallahassee, FL: Findhorn Press, 1997.

Prophet, Elizabeth Clare. *Soul Mates and Twin Flames: The Spiritual Dimension of Love and Relationships*. Corwin Springs, MT: Summit University Press, 1999.

Rashid, Mark. *Horses Never Lie: The Heart of Passive Leadership*. Second Edition, Revised and Updated. New York: Skyhorse Publishing, 2011.

Resnick, Carolyn. *Naked Liberty*. Los Olivos, CA: Amigo Publications, Inc., 2005.

Richo, David. *Shadow Dance: Liberating the Power & Creativity of Your Dark Side*. Boston & London: Shambhala Publications, Inc., 1999.

Ruby, Margaret. *The DNA of Healing: A Five-Step Process For Total Wellness and Abundance*. Charlottesville, VA: Hampton Roads Publishing Company, Inc., 2006.

Ruiz, Don Miguel. *The Four Agreements: A Practical Guide to Personal Freedom*. San Raphael, CA: Amber-Allen Publishing, Inc., 1997.

Roberts, Monte. *The Man Who Listens To Horses: The Story of a Real-Life Horse Whisperer*. New York: Random House, 1997.

Rothschild, Babette. *The Body Remembers: The Psychophysiology of Trauma and Trauma Treatment*. New York: W.W. Norton & Co., Inc., 2000.

Saracino, Laura. "Therapeutic Riding has other benefits for children with autism." Hear Our Voices, October 3, 2012, http://www.blog. hear-our-voices.org/2012/10/03/ therapeutic-riding-has-other-benefits.

Schwartz, Gary, E. Ph.D., with William L. Simon. *The Energy Healing Experiments: Science Reveals Our Natural Power To Heal.* New York: Atria Books, 2007.

Scott, Naomi. *Special Needs, Special Horses: A Guide to the Benefits of Therapeutic Riding.* Denton, TX: University of North Texas, 2005.

Tolle, Eckhart. *A New Earth: Awakening to Your Life's Purpose.* New York: Penguin Group, 2006.

Tompkins, Peter, and Christopher Bird. *The Secret Life of Plants.* New York: HarperCollins, 1973.

Tsu, Lao. *Tao Te Ching,* 25th-Anniversary Edition, Translated by Gia-Fu Feng and Jane English. New York: Vintage Books, 1997.

Virtue, Doreen. *The Care and Feeding of Indigo Children.* Carlsbad, CA: Hay House, Inc., 2001.

_____. *The Crystal Children: A Guide to the Newest Generation of Psychic and Sensitive Children.* Carlsbad, CA: Hay House, Inc., 2003.

Webb, Wyatt. *It's Not About the Horse: It's About Overcoming Fear and Self-Doubt.* Carlsbad, CA: Hay House, 2002.

Williams, Marta. *Beyond Words: Talking With Animals and Nature.* Novato, CA: New World Library, 2005.

_____. *Learning Their Language: Intuitive Communication With Animals and Nature.* Novato, CA: New World Library, 2003.

Wright, Machaelle Small. *Behaving As If the God in All Life Mattered*. Third Edition, Updated and Revised. Warrenton, VA: Perelandra Ltd, 1997.

Yeshe, Lama. *Medicine Dharma Reiki: An Introduction to the Secret Inner Practices*. Delhi, India: Full Circle Publishing, 2002.

ABOUT THE AUTHOR

Heather Green earned a bachelor of science degree in nursing from Clarke College in Dubuque, Iowa, and a master's degree in counseling psychology from Pacifica Graduate Institute in Carpinteria, California. She worked as a registered nurse for thirteen years and a counselor for several years before becoming a human and animal intuitive-healer.

Her articles about horses and spirituality have been published in *The Ojai and Ventura View* newspaper and *Awareness Magazine*. Heather is currently an anchor writer for *Sibyl Magazine: For the Spirit and Soul Of Woman*. She has also guest-lectured about animal communication, healing, spirituality and evolution in humans, and the shift in consciousness on planet Earth for Dreamvisions 7 Radio Network, L.A. Talk Radio, and The Stephanie and Greg Show. She reaches clients worldwide, offering private sessions and classes over the phone and in person. Heather lives on the central coast of California and travels to lecture and hold workshops on animal communication and healing.

To schedule a session or find out about attending or hosting a workshop, please email Heather Green at greenbluehealing@gmail.com or visit her website at www.tealhealing.com.